THE ESSENTIAL BAR BOOK
FOR HOME MIXOLOGISTS

THE ESSENTIAL
BAR
BOOK

· FOR HOME MIXOLOGISTS ·

TOOLS, TECHNIQUES, AND SPIRITS TO MASTER COCKTAILS

AMY TRAYNOR

Illustrations by Tara O'Brien

ROCKRIDGE
PRESS

Interior and Cover Designer: Elizabeth Zuhl
Art Producer: Samantha Ulban
Editor: Gleni Bartels
Illustrations © 2020 Tara O'Brien

ISBN: Print 978-1-64611-715-4 | eBook 978-1-64611-716-1
R0

CONTENTS

Introduction . . . . **viii**

Part I: The Essential Home Bar **1**

    Chapter 1: Essential Equipment **3**

    Chapter 2: Essential Ingredients **11**

    Chapter 3: Essential Techniques **25**

Part II: Entertaining Essentials **33**

    Chapter 4: How to Throw a Cocktail Party Like a Pro **35**

Part III: Essential Recipes 47

    Chapter 5: Vodka 49

    Chapter 6: Rum 65

    Chapter 7: Gin 81

    Chapter 8: Whiskey 97

    Chapter 9: Tequila 113

    Chapter 10: Brandy 127

    Chapter 11: Champagne & Sparkling Wines 139

    Chapter 12: Mocktails 153

Essential Terms 165
A Bartender's Measurement Conversions 168
Measurement Conversions 169
Resources 170
Index 171

INTRODUCTION

If you've ever wanted to become a home mixologist, you might've asked yourself some of the following questions: *What bottles of liquors and liqueurs are truly essential to make my favorite cocktails? Do I really need all that fancy equipment, or will it just sit around collecting dust? How can I throw a cocktail party my friends will remember (for the right reasons)?* Throughout this book, I'll answer these questions and many more—giving you the essential information that will have you mixing drinks like a pro in no time, no matter your budget.

When I was in college, my brother and I moved in together to save money. I had just turned 21 and wanted to explore all of my new boozy drink options. I wasn't a huge fan of beer or wine at the time, so my brother suggested trying a margarita. He pulled out a bottle of tequila, some orange liqueur, and a lime. I couldn't believe that the exquisite cocktail he handed me was made with just three simple ingredients—and it tasted so much better than the margaritas I'd tried to make with a neon-bottled mix! This moment was a major turning point for me, as I suddenly understood that quality, well-crafted cocktails weren't mysterious, difficult elixirs too hard to create at home. And perhaps even more inspiring, I realized that with only a few, relatively inexpensive ingredients, dabbling in home bartending was possible on my limited budget.

Today there are more fancy cocktail and home mixology guidebooks available than ever before, and it can be hard to know which to choose.

Most of the existing books are geared toward advanced audiences, not someone who is looking for just the essentials. The goal of this book is to provide a concise list of the ingredients, tools, and techniques that you'll actually use from day one and can expand upon down the road, rather than an encyclopedia covering all of the options out there.

Over the years, my interest in cocktails and home bartending grew from a hobby into my current role as a full-time cocktail recipe developer and blogger. It took me a long time to develop an understanding of what is truly essential and what you can skip when you're first setting up a home bar. I love helping new home bartenders start small and grow their knowledge before they grow a collection of dusty bottles.

Dipping your toe into the world of craft cocktails can be overwhelming and sometimes intimidating, but with this book as your guide, you can avoid common pitfalls, do more with less, and confidently mix delicious drinks from your first day. Once you've learned the key elements and practiced some of the popular recipes that follow, we'll also cover how to share your home bartending skills with family and friends by throwing a successful cocktail party. So without further ado, let's get mixing! *Cheers!*

The Conception of Cocktails

It's unclear exactly how or when the very first cocktail was invented, but one of the earliest-known cocktails, simply called "Bittered Sling," was little more than spirit, bitters, sugar, and a bit of water. This forefather of the modern Old Fashioned (page 99) was originally intended as a restorative, medicinal tonic.

The term *cocktail* as we know it first appeared in print in 1806 in the *Balance and Columbian Repository* (Hudson, New York). By 1827, the first cocktail book, *Oxford Night Caps*, was published. The book included a selection of popular recipes from the University of Oxford in England, proving that college drinking has a very long history. Decades later, famed bartender Jerry Thomas released his first book, *Bartender's Guide*, a collection of 236 recipes, including some of the best-known cocktails today, like the Mint Julep (page 102), Whiskey Smash (page 105), and Fish House Punch (page 136).

Cocktail culture continued to grow into the 1920s when Prohibition forced drinking underground. During this time, many new cocktails were created to mask the unpleasant flavors of low-quality spirits. After Prohibition, the popularity of cocktails waned for several decades as beer and wine became readily available again. Then, during the 1980s, vodka helped renew interest in cocktails with drinks like the Cosmopolitan (page 51) and Espresso Martini (page 61). Enthusiasm for classic cocktails followed, and a complete craft cocktail renaissance was underway by the early 2000s. Today, both time-honored classics and new and exciting drinks are being created by talented mixologists the world over, and you can join in the booze-fueled fun.

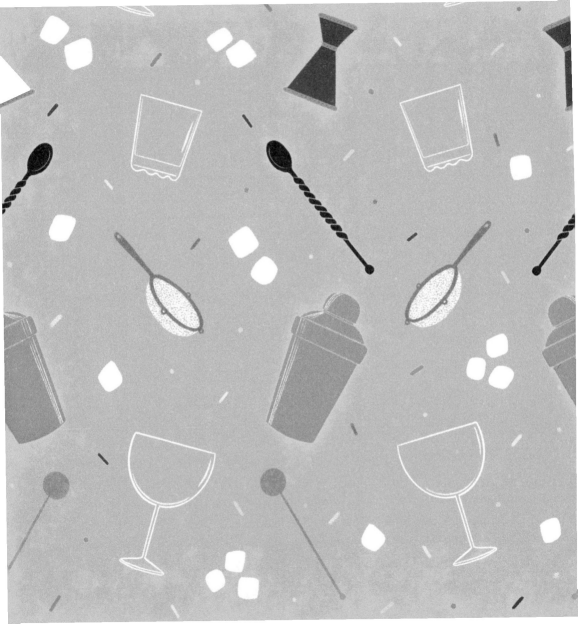

PART I

The Essential Home Bar

In the beginning, start small. Even though each item on your bar serves an important function, many tools can be improvised or purchased inexpensively. I picked up my first Boston shaker set at a thrift shop for two dollars, and the vast majority of my glassware collection has been acquired at similar places for just a few bucks each. When I started, I didn't have much money, so everything I bought had to add a lot of value. In the following chapter, I'll use what I learned to recommend which bottles to buy first, as well as all the tools, equipment, and glassware that you *really* need. I'll also provide helpful hacks so you can make everything from the best-known classic cocktails to contemporary favorites, without breaking the bank.

CHAPTER 1

Essential Equipment

From handmade copper shakers to custom ice molds, there's no shortage of options when it comes to barware. And though these can be fun additions to your collection as your hobby grows, you don't need a lot of fancy products in order to make great cocktails at home. In this chapter, I'll cover what I consider to be the essentials.

THE BAR

When building up a home bar, the first thing you'll need to figure out is, well, the bar itself. You're all set if you have the space for an actual bar top, but you can also make drinks that rival the pros right on your kitchen counter—which is actually where I prepare most of my cocktails.

If you want a dedicated bar area but are limited on square footage, consider buying a bar cart. They're relatively inexpensive and give you a place to prepare drinks, as well as shelves for storage. Plus, they'll almost always have wheels, so you can move them as needed.

Though this book suggests the fewest bottles possible, if you're like me and enjoy adding to your collection regularly, you'll quickly find that this hobby can easily take over your space. To avoid booze creep, designate a cabinet or shelves for storage. Keep in mind that liquors and liqueurs are best stored in cool, dry places, away from direct sunlight, and opened bottles of wines or vermouths should be stored in the refrigerator. Your freezer can act as storage for vodka and gin, too—ice-cold gin and vodka make for great martinis.

TOOLS OF THE TRADE

This list of tools is all you'll need to make the cocktails in this book (and many more!). When you're first getting in the cocktail groove, you can try improvising instead of investing, but a set of quality tools will make crafting consistently great drinks at home quick, easy, and frustration-free.

BAR SPOON: Its long, twisted handle and shallow bowl that's about the volume of one teaspoon makes stirring cocktails and measuring small quantities easy and efficient.

 JIGGER: Perhaps the most essential tool, a jigger allows you to correctly and consistently measure ingredients, which ensures consistently delicious cocktails!

 CITRUS SQUEEZER: Get a cheap, elbow-style citrus squeezer for quick and easy lemon and lime juicing. A citrus reamer works (if you already have one on hand), but squeezers are less messy.

 SHAKER: It's up to you to decide which shaker is your soul mate. The Boston shaker, with its large tin and a mixing glass, can be used as a shaker and a mixing glass. If you opt for a three-piece Cobbler shaker, you'll need to invest in a separate mixing glass for stirred cocktails.

 STRAINER: Easily strain your finished cocktail from the ice it was shaken or stirred in. There are two basic types: the Hawthorne (primarily for shaken drinks) and the Julep (for stirred drinks), though the Hawthorne can work for both needs.

MUDDLER: This long wooden or metal rod has a flat end used for mashing ingredients like fruit or herbs to extract their flavors.

A SHARP KNIFE: A high-quality knife (i.e., sharp!) safely makes quick work of cutting fresh ingredients or peeling citrus for garnishes.

VEGETABLE PEELER (OPTIONAL): Using a Y-style vegetable peeler is the easiest and safest way to peel citrus. You probably have one in your kitchen already, and it's invaluable if you like your cocktails with a twist but don't have great knife skills.

FINE STRAINER (OPTIONAL): Grab one of these only if you enjoy cocktails with muddled ingredients, like the Whiskey Smash (page 105).

BLENDER (OPTIONAL): A blender is only essential if you want to make frozen drinks like the Piña Colada (page 71) or the Scorpion (page 132), but odds are you already have one of these.

Home Bartender Hacks: Tools Edition

No tools, no problem! You can make do with common kitchen items.

Don't have a cocktail shaker? Any large container with a screw-on lid is a great substitute.

Don't have a muddler? Use the end of a thick wooden spoon or a heavy butter knife. Any kitchen tool with a blunt end (spatula, ladle, etc.) can muddle.

Don't have a bar spoon? For measuring, use a teaspoon. For stirring, use any long-handled spoon, a butter knife, or even a chopstick!

Don't have a fine strainer? Use a couple of layers of cheesecloth instead.

Don't have a citrus squeezer or reamer? Use a pair of kitchen tongs. Place the halved fruit inside the inner corner of the tongs, and squeeze.

Don't have a jigger? One tablespoon is equivalent to ½ ounce. Need 2 ounces? That's ¼ cup.

GLASSWARE

Glassware not only adds to the visual appeal of a cocktail but also affects how it tastes. Once you understand different glasses and what kind of cocktails are best suited to each, you can improvise, based on what you have.

 COUPE GLASS: Coupe glasses are often interchangeable with cocktail (or martini) glasses, but they have a smooth, rounded edge that makes them more versatile. They're the vessel of choice for classics like the Daiquiri (page 70).

 ROCKS GLASS: Rocks glasses are stout, heavy-bottomed tumblers used for serving spirits neat or for short cocktails on the rocks, like the Old Fashioned (page 99).

 HIGHBALL: These tall tumblers are used for serving long drinks on ice, like the Tom Collins (page 86).

 CHAMPAGNE FLUTE: The shape of these tall, narrow-stemmed glasses helps keep your French 75 (page 142) bubbly.

Home Bartender Hacks: Glassware Edition

Some drinks can call for specialty items, but do you *really* need them? Nope.

Mint Juleps (page 102) are traditionally served in a silver Julep cup, but you can use a rocks glass instead. Moscow Mules (page 52) taste just as delicious served out of a highball glass as they do out of fancy copper mugs. And if you don't have highball glasses, any high-volume glass can suffice in a pinch. Mason jars are great for tall drinks on ice—or for taking cocktails on the go.

Your red and white wineglasses can pull double duty, too. Small wineglasses can be used in place of rocks glasses—just not for muddling!—and for serving some sparkling wine cocktails. Large wineglasses can serve as highball glasses. In fact, large balloon-style wineglasses are great for Gin and Tonics (page 83), as the rounded glass lets the drinker experience more of the gin's botanical aroma.

One pro tip for any cocktails served up: Chill your glass first by storing it in the freezer or by filling the glass with ice water while you prepare the cocktail. When it's time to strain the drink, toss the ice water and fill your chilled glass. This will help keep the drink cold for as long as possible.

CHAPTER 2

Essential Ingredients

What's actually in a Negroni? Do I really need light and dark rum? Oh god, how much is this going to cost? Don't worry—I promise you don't need to break the bank to have a well-stocked bar. Plus, I've organized the recipe chapters by spirit so you can choose your favorites and grow your collection from there. In this chapter, I'll give a brief rundown of the essential liquors, liqueurs, wines, mixers, and garnishes that will set you up for your craft cocktail journey.

Cleanliness Is Key

Admittedly it's not as fun as enjoying the drink itself, but keeping your tools, ingredients, and bar area clean and organized is as important as using quality ingredients and accurate measurements. I know—after you've fixed a drink, all you want to do is enjoy it, but you'll thank yourself (and me) later if you take some time to give everything a rinse or wipe down. Tools like your shaker, jigger, and citrus squeezer should always get a quick wash with hot, soapy water. Whether I'm making a cocktail, mocktail, or even just seltzer water with lime, my citrus squeezer takes more abuse than any other tool.

You also don't want your bar top (or kitchen counter) and supplies sticky from drips or spills. Aside from just being gross, it could lead to bacteria and germs making their way into your drinks. So trust me and do yourself a favor by wiping down your stuff before you sit down to enjoy that perfectly crafted cocktail.

LIQUORS

At last! The essential liquors that will form the foundation of your well-stocked bar. As a rule of thumb, I suggest starting with midrange bottles when shopping for unfamiliar liquors. Though you don't need the most expensive option, for your taste buds' sake, you'll probably want to avoid anything in an oversized plastic jug located on the bottom shelf. I recommend a few brands at different price points for each liquor, but these are just a starting point. Ultimately your essentials will be a matter of personal taste, so stock favorites you know you'll use, or live dangerously and test out new brands.

VODKA: Vodka is a clear, neutral-tasting distilled spirit most commonly made from cereal grains, potatoes, or fruit. The earliest forms of vodka originated in Russia and Poland during the Middle Ages.
Suggested brands: Tito's Handmade Vodka ($), Absolut ($$), Grey Goose ($$$)

RUM: Rum is a clear or brown spirit made from distilled, fermented sugarcane juice or molasses, which is then aged in oak barrels. Start with a white rum, which will allow you to make a bunch of the classics. When you're ready to grow your collection, add an aged rum to your cocktail repertoire.
Suggested brands: Bacardi ($), Flor de Caña ($), Plantation ($$)

GIN: Gin is a clear distilled spirit made with a variety of botanicals, including the characteristic juniper berry. Gin evolved in England from the Dutch and Belgian liquor Jenever.
Suggested brands: Bombay Sapphire ($), Plymouth ($$), The Botanist ($$)

WHISKEY: Whiskey is a distilled spirit made from fermented grains such as barley, corn, and rye, and is often aged in oak barrels. The first whiskeys date back to Ireland and Scotland during the early Middle Ages. I recommend getting a bottle of bourbon first and adding a bottle of rye whiskey when you're ready to expand your collection. The sidebar on page 103 has more details about whiskey classifications.

Suggested brands: Bulleit ($), Maker's Mark ($$), Woodford Reserve ($$)

TEQUILA: Tequila is a type of mezcal made from distilling fermented blue agave. In order to be tequila, it must be produced only within certain regions in Mexico and according to specific regulations. Page 123 has more info about mezcal.

Suggested brands: Espolòn ($), Tres Agaves ($$), Patrón ($$$)

COGNAC: Cognac is a type of brandy made within the Cognac region of France by distilling white wines according to specific French legal requirements. After distillation, Cognac is aged for at least two years in Limousin oak casks.

Suggested brands: Hennessy VS ($$), Rémy Martin VS ($$), Hine VSOP ($$$)

STORAGE AND SHELF LIFE

Store all bottles of liquor in a cool, dry location away from sunlight. Many spirits can last indefinitely if unopened and stored under ideal conditions, but you'll want to use opened bottles of liquor within six months for best flavor and potency. The one exception here is vodka, which should be used within two years of opening.

Ice, Ice Baby

Ice is an often overlooked but incredibly important element of a craft cocktail. Its role—in all its forms—is twofold: chilling and dilution. No one wants to drink a cocktail that's not cold enough, too strong, or watered down, so be sure to use straight-from-the-freezer ice and plenty of it!

How much ice? For proper chill and dilution making cocktails, aim to fill the shaker or mixing glass about ¾ full of ice.

Cubes: Standard cubes from your freezer are all you need to get started. You can use them to shake, stir, and serve drinks on the rocks.

Crushed: Crushed ice provides extra dilution and extra chill to mixed drinks, and can easily be made at home. Fill a zip-top bag about halfway with ice cubes, press out any excess air, and seal the bag. Wrap the bag in a dish towel and use a mallet or hammer to break the ice into smaller pieces.

Large cubes: Large, two-inch cubes or spheres are all the rage in stirred cocktails. A larger piece of ice melts slower, making for a longer-sipping cocktail.

LIQUEURS

The following liqueurs are essential secondary ingredients for your home bar. They help add flavor, sweetness, and body to craft cocktails. A liqueur begins with a base spirit to which flavoring and sweetener are added. Liqueurs often have lower alcohol content than liquors, although there are exceptions.

TRIPLE SEC: Triple sec is a clear, orange-flavored liqueur that was first created in France in the 1800s. It is often used interchangeably with orange curaçao liqueur, which is an orange liqueur traditionally flavored with the peels of bitter oranges on the island of Curaçao.

Suggested brand: Cointreau ($$)

Used in: Margarita (page 116), Sidecar (page 129), Cosmopolitan (page 51)

CAMPARI ($$): Campari is an Italian bitter liqueur made with a secret blend of botanicals. It is intensely bitter with a characteristic orange flavor. It's also sweet and slightly spicy, making it a popular ingredient in many classic and modern cocktails.

Used in: Negroni (page 87), Boulevardier (page 101), Jungle Bird (page 79)

STORAGE AND SHELF LIFE

Store all liqueurs in a cool, dry place away from direct sunlight. Although the shelf life of liqueurs can vary, depending on the alcohol content and a number of factors, generally speaking, for the best flavor and potency, use liqueurs within one year of opening. If you notice any discoloration or off smell or flavor, just toss the bottle.

FORTIFIED WINES
AND SPARKLING WINES

Wines have a variety of uses in cocktails. Fortified wines are used to add sweetness or herbal flavors to a drink and are often used as modifiers (more on modifiers on page 26). Sparkling wines are often consumed as is, but they are also a key ingredient in many delicious bubbly cocktails.

DRY VERMOUTH: Dry vermouths are white fortified wines flavored with a variety of botanicals. As the name suggests, they aren't very sweet and tend to have a light, somewhat bitter, herbal flavor.

Suggested brands: Noilly Prat ($), Dolin ($)

Used in: Martini (page 89), El Presidente (page 72), Old Pal (page 107)

SWEET VERMOUTH: Sweet vermouths are fortified wines flavored with a variety of botanicals and are red or reddish brown in color. Sweet vermouths have a characteristic sweetness with flavors of baking spices, herbs, and flowers.

Suggested brand: Carpano Antica ($$)

Used in: Boulevardier (page 101), Negroni (page 87), Manhattan (page 100)

SPARKLING WINES: Though sparkling wine often refers to Champagne, in order to be called such, it must be produced according to government regulations within the Champagne region of France. Another sparkling staple is prosecco, an Italian bubbly white wine that can serve as a Champagne substitute.

Suggested Champagne brands: Moët & Chandon ($$), Veuve Clicquot ($$$)

Suggested prosecco brands: Cantine Cavicchioli Prosecco 1928 ($), Mionetto Prosecco Brut ($$)

Used in: Champagne Cocktail (page 141), French 75 (page 142), Death in the Afternoon (page 151)

STORAGE AND SHELF LIFE

Store all fortified and sparkling wines in a cool, dry place away from sunlight. Unopened vermouths can last up to one year under ideal conditions. Once opened, dry vermouth should be refrigerated and will keep for up to three months. Opened sweet vermouth will last for three to six months in the refrigerator. Sparkling wines like Champagne and prosecco should be stored horizontally in a cool, dark location if not being used right away. Non-vintage Champagnes will last for a few years unopened, whereas vintage Champagnes will last 10-plus years. Consume any bubbly within a few days of opening.

MIXERS

Mixers add an important final element to many cocktails. They add balance by sweetening, adding acidity to, or lengthening the drink.

CITRUS JUICES: Fresh citrus juices add sour flavor and acidity to cocktails, helping to balance boozy and sweet flavors.
Examples: lemon, lime, orange, grapefruit

SODAS: Sodas lengthen cocktails, adding dilution, carbonation, and sometimes sweet, bitter, or spicy flavors.

Examples: soda water, tonic water, ginger beer, cola, grapefruit soda

SYRUPS: Cocktail syrups add flavor and sweetness to drinks. Many syrups are very easy to make at home, and others are easy to find at your local liquor or grocery store.

Examples: Simple Syrup (page 85), Honey Syrup (page 75), Berry Syrup (page 159)

STORAGE AND SHELF LIFE

Citrus loses some of its juiciness when chilled, so store any you plan to use within a week or so at room temperature, away from direct sunlight. If you won't be using your fruit right away, store it in the refrigerator, where it can last for three weeks or more.

Store your sodas in the refrigerator so that they are properly chilled for cocktail mixing. They can last a long time unopened, but make sure to check the expiration date before using any that have taken up residence in your refrigerator.

Homemade syrups should be stored in the refrigerator and typically last for about two weeks. The shelf lives of commercial cocktail syrups may vary, so refer to each bottle's storage details and expiration date.

Juice Like a Pro

When it comes to juicing, I prefer an elbow-style citrus squeezer. The fruit should go in cut-side down before squeezing.

The amount of juice you'll get from a fruit will vary, depending on its size and ripeness. The average yields below are for organic citrus, which tends to be smaller with less juice than conventional produce. But no matter what you use, the same tricks apply.

Use the touch and weight tests. Lemons, limes, and grapefruits should have smooth skin and give a little when gently squeezed. Rock-hard lemons and limes with bumpy skin can be much harder to juice and often don't taste as good. When picking oranges, look for fruits that feel heavy for their size, with smooth yet firm skins.

Roll your way to juiciness. To maximize the amount of juice, gently roll lemons and limes back and forth on your counter before cutting them.

Average Juice Yields Per Fruit

LEMON	LIME	ORANGE	GRAPEFRUIT
1 to 2 ounces	½ to 1 ounce	2 to 3 ounces	4 to 6 ounces

GARNISHES AND FLAVORINGS

Using garnishes and flavorings is a simple way to take your cocktails to the next level. They aren't merely fancy finishing touches—they often play a larger role in the drinking experience. It's been said that something like 90 percent of our sense of taste is actually perceived via our sense of smell, and many garnishes add that essential aroma.

ORANGE: One of the most common classic cocktail garnishes, the oils expressed from an orange peel add nuance and brighten the flavors of cocktails like the Old Fashioned (page 99). Orange slices are another classic garnish, adding citrus aroma and a hint of juicy flavor to cocktails like the Aperol Spritz (page 146).

LEMON: The lemon twist gives the orange a run for its money in cocktail garnish popularity. Expressed lemon peels have an almost magical ability to tone down the sweetness of a cocktail, adding a light and fresh acidity. Lemon slices or wheels are perfect complements for refreshing cocktails like the Tom Collins (page 86).

LIME: The humble lime wedge adds an extra burst of fresh citrus flavor to cocktails like the Margarita (page 116) or Moscow Mule (page 52).

MINT: A sprig of mint adds a dimension of cool, fresh, herbal flavor to cocktails like the Mai Tai (page 77). Fresh mint often adds balance by lightening and rounding out heavy, sweet, or sour flavors.

BITTERS: Bitters are concentrated cocktail flavorings made from a variety of botanical ingredients and bittering agents. The most popular brands, Angostura and Peychaud's, are unique flavor blends. Other bitters are just single flavors like orange, cherry, and grapefruit. To get started, pick up a bottle of Angostura bitters, which are used across the board in classic and modern cocktails.

CHAPTER 3

Essential Techniques

Now that we've covered the essential equipment and ingredients, we can talk about how they all come together to make delicious drinks. I'll give some context on the hows and whys of cocktail creation and then go over the skills you'll need to make high-quality craft cocktails at home. When we're done, I'm confident you'll be able to dive into the recipes in this book and whip up something wonderful.

The Anatomy of a Cocktail

Generally speaking, cocktails are composed of three main elements: the base spirit, a modifier, and the seasoning. Let's use the Martini (page 89) as an example: The gin is the base, the vermouth modifies the base, and orange bitters are added to season the overall flavor of the drink.

The **base spirit** is your main liquor. It's also called the "strong" component because it is the main source of alcohol. When creating a recipe, a mixologist seeks to balance the strong flavor of the liquor with other modifying or flavoring ingredients, such as vermouth, citrus, sodas, syrups, or bitters.

Modifiers, sometimes called the "body" of the cocktail, soften the strong flavor of the base and modify without overpowering. Think of it as a supporting role, rather than a lead. The modifier's job is to make the base more enjoyable by adding dilution, texture, or complementary flavors.

The **seasoning** lends a new flavor to the drink or adjusts the flavors of the base and modifier. Think of the seasoning as the salt and pepper of mixology. Rather than adding a whole new layer of flavor, its role is to enhance certain flavors in the base spirit. Proportionately, seasonings are small in quantity, but can transform the way the base and modifiers taste.

COCKTAIL CLASSIFICATIONS

Though there are many ways to classify cocktail recipes, this is how I like to think of the most popular cocktail categories.

OLD FASHIONED: These cocktails gently modify the base spirit and contain only a liquor, sweeteners, and bitters or other seasoning elements. This includes the oldest and simplest drinks like the Old Fashioned (page 99) and the Sazerac (page 108).

SPIRIT FORWARD: These cocktails contain all or mostly alcoholic ingredients like whiskey, vermouth, and bitters. The most common are the Martini (page 89), Manhattan (page 100), and Negroni (page 87).

SOUR: Sours contain a base spirit modified by balanced proportions of sweet and sour ingredients. A classic example is the Margarita (page 116), made with tequila, triple sec, and lime juice.

TIKI OR TROPICAL: These cocktails are typically rum-heavy and incorporate many liqueurs, fruits, or syrups for unique and layered flavors. The Painkiller (page 76) and Jungle Bird (page 79) are good examples.

HIGHBALL: Typically made with a base spirit and a long pour of mixer, these cocktails sometimes get a squeeze of citrus for balance, like the Gin and Tonic (page 83) or the Moscow Mule (page 52).

SHAKE, STIR, AND THEN SOME

These techniques are used to chill and mix cocktail ingredients. Mastering them will help you confidently create just about any cocktail recipe like a pro.

SHAKE: Shaking a drink helps fully incorporate the ingredients and gives a smooth, frothy mouthfeel. Quick, vigorous arm movements ensure the cocktail is both chilled and well mixed. The shaker will become very cold and frost over when the drink is ready, usually about 12 seconds.

DRY-SHAKE: When using egg whites, first shake the ingredients without ice—a "dry-shake"—before adding the ice and shaking to chill the drink. This builds a nice layer of foam and emulsifies all the ingredients for a smooth and creamy texture.

WHIP-SHAKE: For drinks served over crushed ice, add two or three small pieces of ice to the shaker and shake until they dissolve. Then pour the unstrained cocktail into a glass filled with crushed ice. This helps chill the drink without adding too much dilution, since crushed ice will add more water to the finished cocktail than cubed ice.

STIR: To avoid the unnecessary dilution, froth, and air bubbles added by shaking, cocktails with only spirits, liqueurs, or syrups should be stirred for a smooth texture. Put all the ingredients in a mixing glass, fill the glass ¾ full with ice, and stir using a bar spoon until the glass begins to frost over. This takes a bit longer than shaking to reach optimal chill and dilution—aim to stir for about 30 seconds.

MUDDLE: Some cocktails with fresh fruit or herbs require mashing or pressing to release the fresh juices or oils. Using your muddler, press down firmly on the ingredients several times. Mint leaves take on a somewhat bitter flavor when they're crushed, so just lightly press on them to release their oils.

LAYER: If a cocktail requires layering a liqueur or syrup, place your bar spoon against the surface of the finished cocktail, and slowly pour the liquid down the twisted handle. You'll want to pour close to the surface of the cocktail to have the cleanest layers.

THE BELLS AND WHISTLES

A citrus peel or a sprig of mint might make a cocktail a visual showstopper but knowing how to use your ingredients to take your taste buds on a trip is even more important—and can be just as impressive.

PEELING CITRUS: Use a sharp knife or a vegetable peeler to remove a thin strip of peel from your citrus and twist it over your cocktail to release its fragrant oils. Don't remove too much white pith with the peel as it can add an unwanted bitterness when added to a drink.

FLAMING A CITRUS TWIST: This showy garnishing technique adds a smoky or burnt-citrus flavor to the final cocktail. To flame a twist: Light a match, and while holding it near the cocktail, carefully bend or twist the peel to express the oils through the flame and onto the surface of the cocktail.

CLAPPING HERBS: Before adding a fresh herb like mint or thyme to a glass, gently clap the leaves between your hands to release the natural oils.

ADDING BITTERS: Some cocktails are garnished with bitters. Carefully place a few drops on the cocktail's white foam, about an inch apart. If you want to be extra fancy, use a toothpick to draw a continuous line through the drops to make them look like tiny hearts.

RINSING A GLASS: Some spirits with strong flavors, such as absinthe, lend a distinct essence to cocktails. Put a small amount—about ¼ ounce or less—of the alcohol you're rinsing with in your glass. Swirl the glass to coat the inside and then discard the rinse before filling the glass with your finished cocktail.

PART II

Entertaining Essentials

**N**ow that you've mastered all the home bartending basics, it's party time. Literally. Show off your mixology skills to your soon-to-be-amazed family or friends with these cocktail party tips.

CHAPTER 4

How to Throw a Cocktail Party Like a Pro

Your average party prep might involve buying a bunch of booze and chips and hoping for the best, but a *cocktail* party requires a bit of forethought. In this chapter, I'll share my top tips for hosting a classy cocktail shindig, all without spending a ton of time or money.

PARTY PREP

As we've covered in the previous chapters, yes, cocktails will involve a number of ingredients—but if you prepare in advance, you can have your home bar operating as smoothly as your favorite local.

DO'S

START SMALL: Don't try to get everyone you know together all at once to showcase your cocktail-making skills. Once you've got the hang of mixing drinks while hosting, you'll be ready for a larger-scale get-together.

PICK A THEME: This is a great way to get organized. Your theme doesn't have to be complicated; it could be as simple as a tropical vibe with all rum cocktails or a farm-to-table, garden-to-glass theme with all locally sourced ingredients. You can also tailor the theme to your guests, like a spa day with a Mimosa bar and facials.

SET THE MOOD: Once you've established your theme, think about how it will play out in your space. Create a playlist. Buy some simple décor. And don't forget to consider lighting. Candles, string lights, and lanterns are quick ways to give a space ambiance.

Amy's Easy Crostini

Simple canapés are my favorite hors d'oeuvres to serve at any party at any time. Top a small crostini or cracker with two or three layers of complementary or contrasting flavors and textures, and you have a beautiful, delicious snack that's prepared in less than half an hour.

Preheat the oven to 350°F. Place 1 French baguette cut into about 48 (¼-inch-thick) slices in a single layer on a baking sheet and brush both sides with ¼ cup olive oil. Season them with salt and pepper to taste. Bake in batches, if necessary, for 15 to 20 minutes, or until golden, rotating the pan halfway through. Once the crostini are done, allow them to cool before topping. *Makes about 48 crostini*

Some of my go-to toppings include:

- Goat cheese + blueberry jam + a sprig of fresh thyme
- Gorgonzola cheese + fig jam + chopped walnuts
- Gouda cheese + orange marmalade + a fresh raspberry
- Ricotta cheese + sliced fresh strawberries + a drizzle of balsamic vinegar and honey
- Sharp cheddar cheese + apple slices + whole-grain mustard

DON'TS

DON'T FORGET TO ENJOY YOURSELF: If you spend the whole evening cleaning up every empty bottle or plate, you're not spending time with your guests—the whole point of the party!

DON'T FORGET TO BE INCLUSIVE: Consider any dietary restrictions or allergens when creating your menu and remember to have nonalcoholic beverage options. Everyone deserves to have a good time.

DON'T GET DRUNK: It's tempting to keep the drinks flowing when you're having a blast in the comfort of your own home, but do everyone a favor and pace yourself. Stay alert, making sure you and your guests stay hydrated and that anyone who's had a bit too much to drink is either staying put or has a safe ride home.

PARTY SUPPLIES

My number one rule for getting party supplies is: Give yourself time. Spacing out your errands in advance will minimize stress and the number of last-minute panicked text messages to friends about things you forgot. Create a list, broken down into categories, of all necessary supplies, taking into account your theme, the cocktails you plan to serve, and your guests' individual needs and preferences. My timeline usually goes as follows:

NONPERISHABLES: A couple weeks before your party, start picking up things that don't need refrigeration or don't have expiration dates. This can range from things like lighting and décor to chips and jarred salsa, as well as extra glassware or serving ware and cleanup supplies.

ALCOHOL: Next, begin to stock up on the beer, wine, and liquors. These can be purchased in advance but remember to get anything that needs chilling in the refrigerator the night before the party, or if using a cooler, the morning or afternoon before the party.

FRESH FOOD: The week of the party, make a list of what you'll need for the food and see what you can prepare in advance. How far in advance depends on your menu, but I suggest waiting until the day before for fresh items with a short shelf life.

ICE: Lastly, make sure to stock up on your best friend, ice. Have several bags in the freezer and in coolers, depending on your storage situation.

PARTY SETUP

Now that you've got all of your supplies, it's time to start setting up. A few of my favorite hacks include using stemless wineglasses, which are much more stable than their stemmed counterparts, and stocking up on coasters and placing them around the house so people never have an excuse not to use one. Here are a few more tips to make this part easy so you can get to the fun stuff (alcohol).

MAKE SURE YOUR HOME IS *REASONABLY* CLEAN: Don't stress about deep-cleaning every inch, since your guests might make a mess anyway,

How Far Will It Go?

Often the trickiest part of planning a cocktail party is figuring out how much liquor, beer, and wine you'll need. I usually plan for one drink per guest per hour, so a safe bet is three drinks per person for a three- to four-hour party. In broad strokes, there are about 5 glasses of wine in a bottle and 25 ounces of liquor in every 750-mL bottle.

The following chart will help you figure out about how much alcohol to have on hand for an hour of partying, depending on the number of guests you expect.

NUMBER OF GUESTS	5	10	20
WINE	1 bottle	2 bottles	4 bottles
BEER	5 beers	10 beers	20 beers
LIQUOR	10 ounces (just under half a 750-mL bottle)	20 ounces (just under 1 [750-mL] bottle)	40 ounces (just under 2 [750-mL] bottles)

but give the main areas of the party a thorough once-over, making sure anything you don't want out in the open is tucked away.

EMPTY YOUR SINK OR DISHWASHER: Your future self will thank your past self for leaving an empty receptacle for dirty dishes at the end of the party.

USE DÉCOR TO DESIGNATE THE PARTY: Lighting and decorations can help signal which areas are off-limits, which will help keep guests—and messes—contained.

THE PARTY

During the party, it's important to have a good time, but don't forget to be a good host. Here are my top tips to make sure everyone talks about your party for all the right reasons.

MAKE YOUR GUESTS FEEL AT HOME: Do your best as a host to ensure that everyone you invite is comfortable. Introduce your guests to one another. One of the most important but often overlooked elements of an enjoyable party is creating an environment that encourages people to interact. Arrange seating in large, open clusters, rather than small ones, if possible.

GIVE EVERYONE THE CHANCE TO BE FANCY: Have nonalcoholic options that aren't boring bottled water. Set up a self-service water station with pitchers of ice water, wineglasses, and optional add-ins like fresh berries, lemon slices, and mint. These little touches will make hydrating between drinks fun, and nondrinkers won't feel left out.

Common Home Bartending Mistakes

Even the most seasoned bartenders make mistakes, but here are ways to get out in front of some I've seen time and again.

Trying to do too much. I might seem like a broken record, but keeping it simple is truly the easiest path to party success. Don't make a large menu of time-consuming cocktails. Select one or two drinks made to order or go with batched cocktails.

Free pouring. If you don't want your guests making faces after a sip, always measure your ingredients. It'll ensure delicious cocktails every time.

Not shaking or stirring for long enough. If you don't shake or stir until your vessel frosts over, your drinks won't be cold enough and they'll taste too strong.

Not having or using enough ice. Ice is sometimes an after-thought, but it should be your VIP. It's an integral party ingredient, whether it's for making cocktails or keeping beverages cold. Always make sure to have a bag or two more than you think you'll need.

BATCH COCKTAILS IN ADVANCE: If you don't want to be stuck behind the bar making drinks all night, opt for batched cocktails. (I've got some options on pages 58, 118, and 137.) If you still want to show off those cocktail-making skills, choose two or three signature cocktails that you'll be shaking or stirring for the party. Fewer options will mean quicker drink prep and more time spent socializing.

THE AFTER-PARTY

Now that the party's over, you're left with the cleanup and storage of leftovers. Plan for these tasks in advance and save yourself a major headache.

DO A FIVE-MINUTE CLEANUP: No matter how late the party ends, take a few minutes to tidy up. Bring dishes and glassware to the kitchen, gather any garbage or recycling, and quickly organize whatever's within reach. Taking the time to do this while still riding your party high will make the next day much easier (especially if you have a party hangover).

STORE LEFTOVER WINE AND BEER: Refrigerate all opened wines. If your refrigerator is full of party snacks, store unopened beer in a cool, dark place like the back of a closet or the basement. Don't worry about keeping it cold. Allowing cold beer to warm to room temperature and then chilling it again will not "skunk" or ruin it. This is only true if it's exposed to multiple rounds of extreme temperature fluctuations.

Hangover Cures
from Someone Who Knows

We've all been there. You tried to pace your drinking, but red wine led to shots of tequila … and now you're the proud owner of a raging hangover. Although there's no real instant cure, I've found a few things that can help me feel better faster.

Sleep. Perhaps most important of all: Make sure you're going to be able to get enough sleep. If you don't get enough rest, you're going to feel a lot worse.

Hydrate. Make sure you're drinking plenty of water between rounds, and as soon as you wake up—whether in the morning or in the middle of the night—try to immediately start drinking fluids. Water is best, but personally I can't tolerate plain water first thing in the morning when I'm nauseous. I like to start with Gatorade or a mix of juice and seltzer to help settle my stomach.

Carbs, fat, protein. The sooner I can eat some solid food, the sooner things start to turn around. Everyone seems to have their own food-based hangover remedies, but a meal with carbs, protein, and some fat—like a bacon, egg, and cheese breakfast sandwich—has never let me down.

Hair of the dog. If all else fails, have a Bloody Mary (page 54). An ounce or two of vodka can help boost endorphins, which makes your hangover symptoms easier to cope with, and the nutrients in the tomato or vegetable juice might help speed up your recovery. You could also try one of the Corpse Revivers (pages 94 and 134).

In Harry Craddock's *The Savoy Cocktail Book,* he hilariously notes of the Corpse Reviver #2: "Four of these taken in swift succession will unrevive the corpse again." I'd recommend having just one . . . or you might find yourself in need of further reviving later on.

Essential Recipes

The best part of setting up and stocking a home bar is having top-notch cocktails always at your fingertips. The following cocktails range from vintage to modern, with some you'll recognize right away and others that will soon be new go-to drinks. The majority use only the essential ingredients, tools, and techniques covered in part one, but I've included some more complex recipes and given guidance on what to buy next as your home bar grows. The following chapters are organized by type of alcohol so you can easily flip to your favorite spirit, and all recipes yield one cocktail, though some have directions on how to make a bigger batch.

CHAPTER 5

Vodka

Vodka's neutral flavor has helped make it the spirit of choice in some of the world's most popular cocktails. From the savory Bloody Mary to the refreshingly spicy Moscow Mule, there's a vodka cocktail to suit every taste.

Cosmopolitan	**51**		Lemon Drop	**56**
Moscow Mule	**52**		Caipirovska	**57**
Cape Codder	**53**		Russian Spring Punch	**58**
Bloody Mary	**54**		Espresso Martini	**61**
Easy Bloody Mary Mix	**55**		Bernice	**62**

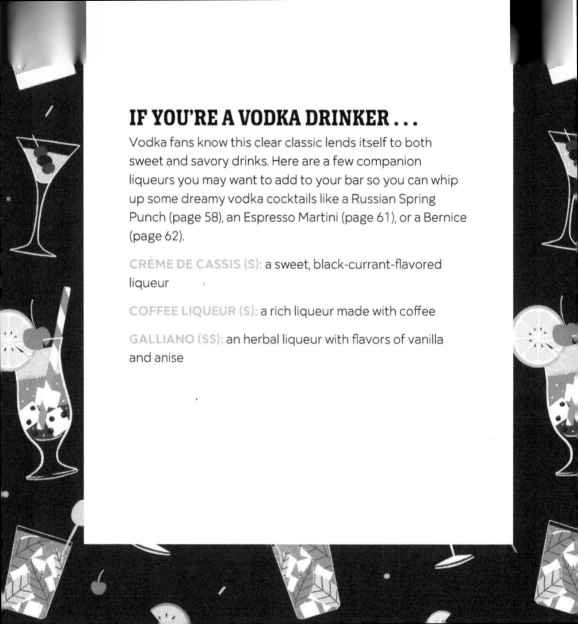

IF YOU'RE A VODKA DRINKER . . .

Vodka fans know this clear classic lends itself to both sweet and savory drinks. Here are a few companion liqueurs you may want to add to your bar so you can whip up some dreamy vodka cocktails like a Russian Spring Punch (page 58), an Espresso Martini (page 61), or a Bernice (page 62).

CRÈME DE CASSIS ($): a sweet, black-currant-flavored liqueur

COFFEE LIQUEUR ($): a rich liqueur made with coffee

GALLIANO ($$): an herbal liqueur with flavors of vanilla and anise

Cosmopolitan

Tools: knife, jigger, citrus squeezer, shaker, strainer

The Cosmopolitan first appeared in the 1980s, but its biggest claim to fame is being the drink of choice for the women of *Sex and the City*. The Cosmopolitan is essentially a Kamikaze, another popular cocktail, with a splash of sweet and tart cranberry juice.

2 ounces vodka

¾ ounce cranberry juice cocktail

¾ ounce freshly squeezed lime juice

¾ ounce triple sec

Orange twist, for garnish

Combine the vodka, cranberry juice, lime juice, and triple sec in a cocktail shaker. **Fill** the shaker ¾ full with ice cubes and shake for about 12 seconds, or until chilled. **Strain** the liquid into your glass and garnish with an orange twist.

VODKA

Moscow Mule

Tools: knife, jigger, citrus squeezer, bar spoon

The Moscow Mule has enjoyed a surge in popularity in recent years, but it was born in the 1940s. There are several stories about how the Moscow Mule first came to be, but most attribute its invention to a creative use of overstock vodka and ginger beer.

2 ounces vodka

½ ounce freshly squeezed lime juice

6 ounces ginger beer

Lime wheel, for garnish

Fill your glass with ice cubes. **Add** the vodka and lime juice and stir a few times to chill. **Top** with the ginger beer and garnish with a lime wheel on the rim.

❂ You can make a Mule (also traditionally called "Buck"-style cocktails) with any of the spirits listed in this book! Simply swap out the vodka for another liquor of choice.

Cape Codder

Tools: knife, jigger, bar spoon

The Cape Codder is another name for the classic two-ingredient cocktail the Vodka-Cranberry. If you're short on time or ingredients, this is one of the easiest drinks to mix up for one or for a group.

2 ounces vodka

4 ounces cranberry juice cocktail

Lime wedge

Fill a rocks glass with ice cubes. **Add** the vodka and cranberry juice and stir several times to chill. **Squeeze** the lime wedge over the cocktail and drop it into the glass.

Batch it: Multiply the recipe by the number of drinks you need. Put the vodka and cranberry juice in a pitcher. Stir well to combine and chill in the refrigerator for a few hours before serving. Serve over ice in rocks glasses and garnish each with a lime wedge.

VODKA

Bloody Mary

Tools: knife, jigger, citrus squeezer, bar spoon

Invented in the 1920s, the Bloody Mary was the first cocktail to popularize vodka. You can easily make your own Easy Bloody Mary Mix (page 55) at home or purchase premade mixes at your local liquor or grocery store. There are many quality mixes on the market today, and some of my favorites are Bloody Gerry and Cocktail Artist.

2 ounces vodka

½ ounce freshly squeezed lemon juice

6 ounces Bloody Mary mix

Celery stalk, for garnish

Fill a highball glass with ice cubes. **Add** the vodka, lemon juice, and Bloody Mary mix and stir several times to chill. **Garnish** with a celery stalk, which you can use to gently stir the cocktail if any spices begin to settle at the bottom.

🍸 When garnishing a Bloody Mary, you don't have to stop at a lone celery stalk. It's common to see them garnished to the nines with savory and spicy finger foods. Some of my favorite Bloody Mary garnishes (read: snacks) include barbecue ribs, chicken wings, and any assortment of olives, peppers, or pickled vegetables.

Easy Bloody Mary Mix

Everyone has their own preferences when it comes to how a Bloody Mary is seasoned, and this easy mix is a great starting point. Feel free to adjust the hot sauce and horseradish to your own taste or allow your guests to add those ingredients themselves. For maximum flavor, choose a vegetable juice blend over a basic tomato juice.

32 ounces tomato juice or tomato and vegetable juice blend

1¼ teaspoons Worcestershire sauce

¾ teaspoon hot sauce

½ teaspoon black pepper

¼ teaspoon celery salt

Prepared horseradish (optional)

Combine the tomato juice, Worcestershire sauce, hot sauce, black pepper, celery salt, and horseradish to taste (if using) in a large pitcher, and stir thoroughly. **Store** covered in the refrigerator for up to a week. *Makes 5 drinks*

VODKA

Lemon Drop

Tools: knife, jigger, citrus squeezer, shaker, strainer

The Lemon Drop is an easy-to-love, sweet-and-sour cocktail. It was invented sometime in the 1970s but didn't reach its height of popularity until the 1990s when it was commonly served in short form as a shooter. Skip the shot glasses and try the Lemon Drop as it was meant to be enjoyed, in a classy cocktail glass complete with sugared rim.

2 tablespoons sugar, for the rim

Lemon wedge, for the rim

2 ounces vodka

1 ounce triple sec

1 ounce freshly squeezed lemon juice

Put the sugar in a shallow dish. **Rub** a lemon wedge along the rim of your glass. **Dip** the rim of the glass into the sugar at an angle, one side at a time, keeping the sugar on the outside rim. **Combine** the vodka, triple sec, and lemon juice in a cocktail shaker. **Fill** the shaker ¾ full with ice cubes and shake for about 12 seconds, or until chilled. **Strain** the cocktail into the sugar-rimmed glass.

Caipirovska

Tools: knife, jigger, muddler, bar spoon

The Caipirovska is a variation on the classic Brazilian cocktail the Caipirinha. Vodka is used in place of Brazil's native spirit, cachaça. This cocktail is very easy to make and requires just a few simple ingredients, making it a great option for beginner home bartenders.

½ lime, cut into wedges

2 teaspoons sugar

2 ounces vodka

Put the lime wedges and sugar in a rocks glass and muddle thoroughly. **Fill** the glass with ice cubes, add the vodka, and stir about 20 times to chill.

🍸 You can substitute ½ ounce Simple Syrup (page 85) in place of the sugar, if you have some on hand.

Russian Spring Punch

Tools: knife, jigger, citrus squeezer, shaker, strainer

The Russian Spring Punch was invented by famed bartender Dick Bradsell in the 1980s for a friend's cocktail party. Although the original recipe called for crème de cassis (black currant liqueur), some variations call for raspberry liqueur, which may be easier to find. With a combination of vodka, liqueur, and sparkling wine, this pretty cocktail is stronger than she looks.

1 ounce vodka

½ ounce freshly squeezed lemon juice

¼ ounce crème de cassis

¼ ounce Simple Syrup (page 85)

3 ounces sparkling wine

Lemon wheel, for garnish

Fresh raspberries or blackberries, for garnish

Combine the vodka, lemon juice, crème de cassis, and simple syrup in a cocktail shaker. **Fill** the shaker ¾ full with ice cubes and shake for about 12 seconds, or until chilled. **Fill** a highball glass with ice and strain the liquid into the glass. **Top** with the sparkling wine. **Garnish** with a lemon wheel and fresh berries before serving.

Batch it: Chill your bottles overnight. On the day of the party, juice enough lemons to have ½ ounce of fresh juice per guest (see page 20). Refrigerate the juice until 10 to 20 minutes before serving. To each highball glass, add 1 ounce vodka, ½ ounce lemon juice, ¼ ounce crème de cassis, and ¼ ounce simple syrup. Fill each glass with ice, top with sparkling wine, and garnish with a lemon wheel and fresh berries. Serve with a straw.

VODKA

Famous Bartenders:
Dick Bradsell

Dick Bradsell (Richard Arthur Bradsell) was born in Bishop's Stortford, England, on May 4, 1959. Bradsell was an innovative London bartender who created many cocktails during the 1980s that have become modern classics. Some of Bradsell's best-known drinks include the Espresso Martini (page 61), Bramble (page 91), and Russian Spring Punch (page 58). Tragically, Bradsell died from brain cancer in 2016.

Espresso Martini

Tools: jigger, shaker, strainer

The Espresso Martini is another modern classic that was invented by London bartender Dick Bradsell in the 1980s. A popular story about the origin of the cocktail is that supermodel Kate Moss requested a drink that would both wake her up and give her a buzz.

1½ ounces vodka

1 ounce freshly brewed espresso

1 ounce coffee liqueur

Coffee beans, for garnish (optional)

Combine the vodka, espresso, and coffee liqueur in a cocktail shaker. **Fill** the shaker ¾ full with ice cubes and shake for about 12 seconds, or until chilled. **Strain** the cocktail into your glass, and garnish with coffee beans (if using).

Bernice

Tools: knife, jigger, citrus squeezer, shaker, strainer

The Bernice is a 1950s cocktail made with the vanilla-and-anise-flavored liqueur, Galliano. The Bernice is essentially an herbal variation of the Gimlet (page 84), which is a mix of vodka or gin with lime juice and simple syrup. This cocktail first appeared in Ted Saucier's 1951 cocktail book, *Bottoms Up*.

2 ounces vodka

¾ ounce freshly squeezed lime juice

¼ ounce Galliano

½ ounce Simple Syrup (page 85)

Mint leaf, for garnish

Combine the vodka, lime juice, Galliano, and simple syrup in a cocktail shaker. **Fill** the shaker ¾ full with ice cubes and shake for about 12 seconds, or until chilled. **Strain** the cocktail into a coupe glass and garnish with a mint leaf.

CHAPTER 6

Rum

Rum was the spirit of choice for early American colonists, and it's said that about 4 gallons were consumed per person per year. Even George Washington used rum's popularity to his advantage, serving copious amounts of rum and rum punch at political events to secure votes in his favor.

Cuba Libre **67**

Mojito. **68**

Daiquiri **70**

Piña Colada. **71**

El Presidente. **72**

Dark 'n' Stormy **73**

Missionary's Downfall. **74**

Honey Syrup **75**

Painkiller **76**

Mai Tai **77**

Jungle Bird **79**

IF YOU'RE A RUM DRINKER . . .

If you're a rum-loving pirate at heart, consider adding these bottles and ingredients to your home bar. They'll be handy for mixing such beloved rum cocktails as the Mai Tai (page 77), El Presidente (page 72), and Missionary's Downfall (page 74).

AGED RUM ($ TO $$$): rums that have been barrel-aged for at least three years and possess a deep golden or brown color and a rich, full-bodied flavor

GRENADINE ($): a sweet and tart pomegranate-flavored syrup

ORGEAT ($): a syrup made from almonds and a hint of orange blossom water

PEACH LIQUEUR ($): a peach-flavored liqueur

Cuba Libre

Tools: knife, jigger, citrus squeezer, bar spoon

The Cuba Libre is a fancier name for the beloved Rum and Coke. This simple cocktail is improved greatly by using a quality rum and a generous squeeze of fresh lime juice.

2 ounces white rum

½ ounce freshly squeezed lime juice

4 ounces cola soda

Lime wheel, for garnish

Fill a highball glass with ice cubes. **Add** the rum and lime juice and stir several times to chill. **Fill** the glass with the cola and garnish with a lime wheel.

✧ Try making the Cuba Libre with Mexican Coca-Cola. Mexican Coke is made with sugar (instead of corn syrup) and packaged in glass, and some say these qualities give it better taste and carbonation.

Mojito

Tools: knife, shaker, muddler, jigger, citrus squeezer, strainer

The Mojito is one of the best-known rum cocktails. It's unclear when this Cuban cocktail was first created, but author Ernest Hemingway helped popularize it in the United States. Light and refreshing, the Mojito blends white rum with lime, mint, and soda water.

8 to 10 fresh mint leaves, divided

2 ounces white rum

¾ ounce freshly squeezed lime juice

½ ounce Simple Syrup (page 85)

Soda water

Mint sprig, for garnish

Lime wheel, for garnish

Put all but one mint leaf in a cocktail shaker and press on the leaves a few times with a muddler. **Add** the rum, lime juice, and simple syrup to the shaker, and fill ¾ full with ice cubes. **Shake** the mixture for about 12 seconds, or until chilled. **Fill** a highball glass with ice cubes. **Fine-strain** the liquid into the glass filled with ice cubes and top with soda water. **Garnish** with a sprig of mint and a lime wheel.

Batch it: Multiply the recipe by the number of drinks you need. In a large pitcher, combine the mint and lime juice and gently press with a muddler a few times. Pour in the rum and simple syrup and stir several times to combine. Chill for at least a few hours or add ice to the pitcher and stir to chill. Fill highball glasses with ice and pour about 3 ounces into each glass. Top with soda water and garnish.

Daiquiri

Tools: knife, jigger, citrus squeezer, shaker, strainer

A far cry from the overly sweet slushies that have come to be associated with the name, the classic Daiquiri is simple and perfectly balanced. The story goes that the Daiquiri was invented at a party in Cuba in the late 1800s when the host ran out of gin.

2 ounces white rum

1 ounce freshly squeezed lime juice

¾ ounce Simple Syrup (page 85)

Combine the rum, lime juice, and simple syrup in a cocktail shaker. **Fill** the cocktail shaker ¾ full with ice cubes and shake for about 12 seconds, or until chilled. **Strain** the cocktail into a coupe glass.

🍸 Make it a Strawberry Daiquiri by muddling a few fresh strawberries in your cocktail shaker before adding the remaining ingredients. Just be sure to fine-strain the drink when serving to prevent any fruit from ending up in your glass.

Piña Colada

Tools: knife, jigger, citrus squeezer, blender

It's up for debate who first created this iconic tropical cocktail, but the Piña Colada first appeared in Puerto Rico sometime during the 1950s. This delicious blend of rum, pineapple, coconut, and lime is not overly sweet when made properly, making it the perfect beach-time or poolside sip.

2 ounces white rum

3 ounces pineapple juice

1 ounce cream of coconut

½ ounce freshly squeezed lime juice

Pineapple wedge, for garnish

Cocktail cherry, for garnish

Combine the rum, pineapple juice, cream of coconut, and lime juice in a blender. **Add** ¾ cup of crushed ice and blend on high speed until smooth. **Pour** the cocktail into your glass and garnish with a wedge of pineapple and a cocktail cherry.

El Presidente

THE ESSENTIAL BAR BOOK FOR HOME MIXOLOGISTS

Tools: jigger, mixing glass, bar spoon, strainer

This stirred rum cocktail rose to fame in the 1920s in Cuba, where it was allegedly created in honor of then-president Mario García Menocal. In recent times, the drink was typically made with dry vermouth until cocktail historian David Wondrich discovered that the original recipe called for blanc-style vermouth. If you'd like to add it to your collection, blanc vermouth is a clear, French vermouth that is slightly sweet and can transform the character of this classic drink.

1½ ounces white rum

1½ ounces dry vermouth

1 bar spoon triple sec

1 bar spoon grenadine

Cocktail cherry, for garnish

Combine the rum, vermouth, triple sec, and grenadine in a mixing glass. **Fill** the mixing glass ¾ full with ice and stir for about 30 seconds, or until chilled. **Strain** the cocktail into a coupe glass and garnish with a cocktail cherry.

Dark 'n' Stormy

Tools: knife, jigger

The Dark 'n' Stormy was invented in Bermuda around 1860 when British sailors began mixing ginger beer with Gosling's rum. Today the cocktail is trademarked by Gosling's, and the use of the famous name requires that the cocktail be made with Gosling's ingredients. Of course, other rums and ginger beers can be substituted, but the drink is no longer a true Dark 'n' Stormy.

RUM

4 ounces ginger beer

1½ ounces aged rum

Lime wedge, for garnish

Fill a highball glass with ice cubes. **Add** the ginger beer and top with the rum. **Garnish** with a lime wedge.

Missionary's Downfall

Tools: knife, shaker, muddler, jigger, citrus squeezer, strainer

The Missionary's Downfall was first created at the Don the Beachcomber restaurant in California in the 1930s. This fruity, herbal, and refreshing rum drink combines pineapple, lime, peach, and mint for a uniquely delicious tropical cocktail.

10 mint leaves

1½ ounces white rum

1 ounce pineapple juice

¾ ounce freshly squeezed lime juice

½ ounce peach liqueur

½ ounce Honey Syrup (page 75)

Mint sprig, for garnish

Put the mint leaves in a cocktail shaker and press on them a few times with a muddler. **Add** the rum, pineapple juice, lime juice, liqueur, and honey syrup. **Whip-shake** the cocktail by adding a few ice cubes to the shaker and shaking until the ice cubes dissolve. **Fill** a highball glass with crushed ice. **Strain** the cocktail into the glass filled with crushed ice and garnish with a sprig of mint.

Honey Syrup

Honey syrup is a blend of equal parts honey and water. On its own, honey is thick and does not mix well into cold drinks. When loosened with water, it incorporates quickly and easily into cocktails or other drinks.

½ cup water
½ cup honey

Combine the water and honey in a sealable container, and stir for about 1 minute, or until the honey dissolves. **Store** the syrup in the refrigerator for up to two weeks. *Makes ½ cup*

Painkiller

Tools: knife, jigger, citrus squeezer, shaker, strainer, grater

Also known as Pusser's Painkiller, this tropical cocktail made with rum, pineapple, coconut, and orange is the signature drink of Pusser's Rum, though you can use any dark rum you have on hand. The sweet and creamy nature of the cocktail makes it dangerously easy to drink.

2 ounces dark rum

4 ounces pineapple juice

1 ounce freshly squeezed orange juice

1 ounce cream of coconut

Freshly grated nutmeg, for garnish

Combine the rum, pineapple juice, orange juice, and cream of coconut in a cocktail shaker. **Fill** the shaker ¾ full with ice cubes and shake for about 12 seconds, or until chilled. **Fill** your glass with ice cubes. **Strain** the cocktail into the glass and garnish with a sprinkling of freshly grated nutmeg.

Mai Tai

Tools: knife, jigger, citrus squeezer, shaker

The Mai Tai is one of the most famous tropical, or "tiki"-style, cocktails. The origin of the cocktail's name is said to be the Tahitian word *maita'i*, meaning *good*.

2 ounces aged rum

¾ ounce freshly squeezed lime juice

½ ounce triple sec

¼ ounce orgeat

Mint sprig, for garnish

Combine the rum, lime juice, triple sec, and orgeat in a cocktail shaker. **Whip-shake** the cocktail by adding a few ice cubes and shaking until the cubes dissolve. **Fill** a rocks glass with crushed ice. **Pour** the cocktail into the glass and garnish with a sprig of mint.

RUM

It's Tiki Time!

When you think of the word *tiki*, you probably think of tropical décor and rum-based drinks served in bright, fun glasses with paper umbrellas.

You're not wrong, but did you know that tiki bars and restaurants first became popular way back in the 1930s to give people an exotic, immersive escape from their everyday lives? In 1934, Donn the Beachcomber opened his first restaurant in LA, and a few years later Trader Vic opened his first bar.

Both men (who famously feuded over who created the original Mai Tai) used the knowledge they gained from their extensive overseas travels to bring the influences of Polynesia and the Caribbean back to America—not only in the décor but also in the complex, blended flavors of the drinks they served. Like a vacation in a glass, the hotly debated Mai Tai on page 77 is a great example of a classic tiki drink.

Jungle Bird

Tools: knife, jigger, citrus squeezer, shaker

The Jungle Bird was created in 1973 in Malaysia by bartender Jeffrey Ong and later rose to international fame after being featured in the book *Intoxica!* by Jeff "Beachbum" Berry. The Jungle Bird is an unexpectedly refreshing tiki cocktail, combining rum and pineapple with the bittersweet liqueur Campari.

1½ ounces aged rum

1½ ounces pineapple juice

¾ ounce Campari

½ ounce Simple Syrup (page 85)

½ ounce freshly squeezed lime juice

Pineapple wedge, for garnish

Cocktail cherry, for garnish

Combine the rum, pineapple juice, Campari, simple syrup, and lime juice in a cocktail shaker. **Whip-shake** the cocktail by adding a few ice cubes and shaking until the cubes dissolve. **Fill** a rocks glass with crushed ice. **Pour** the cocktail into the glass and garnish with a wedge of pineapple and a cocktail cherry.

CHAPTER 7

Gin

G in has experienced a massive revival in recent years, but it wasn't always seen as a base for crisp, trendy cocktails. During the "Gin Craze" of the early 1700s, gin consumption was so out of control in Great Britain that Parliament passed several acts to try to curb public drunkenness and the bad behavior it often led to.

Gin and Tonic **83**

Gimlet **84**

Simple Syrup **85**

Tom Collins **86**

Negroni **87**

Jasmine **88**

Martini **89**

Clover Club **90**

Bramble **91**

Hanky Panky **92**

Corpse Reviver #2 . . . . **94**

Ramos Gin Fizz **95**

IF YOU'RE A GIN DRINKER . . .

If you like your cocktails crisp and classy, with just a hint of pine tree, odds are you're a gin fan. Consider stocking up on these bottles and ingredients so you can make all the classic gin drinks, from a Ramos Gin Fizz (page 95) to a Gin Martini (page 89).

ABSINTHE ($$): a potent spirit made with a blend of botanicals, including wormwood, anise, and fennel

FERNET BRANCA ($$): a strongly flavored, herbal, bitter-sweet liqueur with a secret blend of 27 botanicals

LILLET BLANC ($): a French aromatized wine made with Bordeaux wines and a blend of sweet and bitter orange liqueurs

ORANGE BITTERS ($): a concentrated cocktail flavoring typically made with orange peels and a blend of spices in a base of either alcohol or glycerine

ORANGE BLOSSOM WATER ($): a floral-scented water created as a by-product of bitter orange essential oil production

Gin and Tonic

Tools: knife, jigger, citrus squeezer, bar spoon

The Gin and Tonic was famously invented by British soldiers looking for a way to make their anti-malaria tonic more palatable. Since its creation in the late 1880s, the Gin and Tonic has remained a very popular gin cocktail.

2 ounces gin

½ ounce freshly squeezed lime juice

4 to 6 ounces tonic water

Lime wedge, for garnish

Fill a highball glass with ice cubes. **Add** the gin and lime juice and stir several times to chill. **Fill** the glass with tonic water and garnish with a lime wedge.

🍸 Try experimenting with different aromatic garnishes to suit the botanical profile of your gin. Some options are fresh mint, rosemary, lemon, grapefruit, or pink peppercorn.

Gimlet

Tools: knife, jigger, citrus squeezer, shaker, strainer

The Gimlet is a classic gin cocktail that dates back to at least the late 1800s. Many stories claim that the drink was first concocted as an anti-scurvy tonic for British sailors. Traditionally made with just gin and Rose's Lime Cordial, modern recipes call for a less sweet, more balanced mix of fresh lime juice and simple syrup.

2 ounces gin

¾ ounce freshly squeezed lime juice

¾ ounce Simple Syrup (page 85)

Lime wheel, for garnish

Combine the gin, lime juice, and simple syrup in a cocktail shaker. **Fill** the shaker ¾ full with ice cubes and shake for about 12 seconds, or until chilled. **Strain** the cocktail into a coupe glass and garnish with a lime wheel.

🍸 Try a traditional Gimlet by shaking 2 ounces of gin with 1 ounce of Rose's Lime Cordial (sometimes also called Rose's Sweetened Lime Juice).

Simple Syrup

Simple syrup is simply a mixture of equal parts sugar and water. Many simple syrup recipes call for hot water, but it's not necessary to heat the water, and if you boil your syrup, you alter its level of sweetness as the water boils off. This means that each batch of syrup you make may be slightly more or less sweet, which will affect how your cocktails taste.

1 cup water
1 cup sugar

Combine the water and sugar in a resealable container, and stir for 2 to 3 minutes, or until the sugar dissolves. **Store** the syrup in the refrigerator for up to two weeks. You can add an ounce of vodka to the syrup to help it keep longer. *Makes about 1½ cups*

Tom Collins

Tools: knife, jigger, citrus squeezer, shaker, strainer

The Tom Collins drinks like gin-spiked, sparkling lemonade. The original was made with Old Tom gin, which is slightly sweetened. Today, it's common to use a classic London dry gin.

2 ounces gin

1 ounce freshly squeezed lemon juice

1 ounce Simple Syrup (page 85)

Soda water

Lemon wheel, for garnish

Cocktail cherry, for garnish

Combine the gin, lemon juice, and simple syrup in a cocktail shaker. **Fill** the shaker ¾ full with ice cubes and shake for about 12 seconds, or until chilled. **Fill** your glass with ice cubes. **Strain** the cocktail into the glass and top with soda water. **Garnish** with a lemon wheel and a cocktail cherry.

🍷 If you choose to use Old Tom gin, reduce the simple syrup to ½ ounce.

Batch it: Multiply the recipe by the number of drinks needed. Put the gin, lemon juice, and simple syrup in a large pitcher and stir. Shortly before serving, add ice, and stir to chill. Fill each highball glass with ice and about 4 ounces of cocktail. Top with soda water and garnish.

Negroni

Tools: knife, jigger, mixing glass, bar spoon, strainer

Of all the vintage cocktails to experience renewed interest in recent years, the Negroni may be the best known. This intense, bright red cocktail is bold, bitter, and boozy. The Negroni is named for its alleged creator, Italian Count Camillo Negroni. Legend has it that the count asked his bartender to make a boozier Milano-Torino (known today as an Americano) by adding gin instead of club soda to the drink.

1 ounce gin

1 ounce Campari

1 ounce sweet vermouth

Orange twist, for garnish

Combine the gin, Campari, and vermouth in a mixing glass. **Fill** the mixing glass ¾ full with ice cubes and stir for about 30 seconds, or until chilled. **Fill** a rocks glass with ice or use one large ice cube. **Strain** the cocktail into the glass and garnish with an orange twist.

Jasmine

Tools: knife, jigger, citrus squeezer, shaker, strainer

The Jasmine is a light, not-too-sweet gin cocktail that was invented in the 1990s by American bartender Paul Harrington. A quarter ounce of the bitter liqueur Campari gives this cocktail its lovely pink hue and a pleasantly bittersweet flavor.

1½ ounces gin

¾ ounce freshly squeezed lemon juice

¼ ounce Campari

¼ ounce triple sec

Lemon twist, for garnish

Combine the gin, lemon juice, Campari, and triple sec in a cocktail shaker. **Fill** the shaker ¾ full with ice cubes and shake for about 12 seconds, or until chilled. **Strain** the cocktail into a coupe glass and garnish with a lemon twist.

Martini

Tools: knife, jigger, mixing glass, bar spoon, strainer

The iconic Martini has seen many variations over the years, with a tendency toward too large and too dry since the 1980s. Try this classic ratio instead, and see why dry vermouth plays a critical role in this simple, savory cocktail.

2½ ounces gin

½ ounce dry vermouth

2 dashes orange bitters

Lemon twist or olive, for garnish

Combine the gin, vermouth, and bitters in a mixing glass. **Fill** the mixing glass ¾ full with ice cubes, and stir for about 30 seconds, or until chilled. **Strain** the cocktail into your glass, and garnish with a lemon twist or an olive.

Batch it: Multiply the recipe by the number of drinks you need. Put the gin, vermouth, bitters, and ½ ounce water for each serving in a large pitcher. Stir to combine, and chill in the refrigerator for at least a few hours prior to serving. Serve in chilled glasses, and garnish with either lemon twists or olives.

GIN

Clover Club

Tools: knife, jigger, citrus squeezer, shaker, strainer

The Clover Club is a classic gin cocktail named for a Philadelphia men's club. This beautiful pink and white cocktail is flavored with rasberry syrup and uses egg white for a smooth and creamy finish.

1½ ounces gin

½ ounce dry vermouth

½ ounce freshly squeezed lemon juice

½ ounce Berry Syrup (see page 159)

1 large egg white

3 raspberries, for garnish

Combine the gin, vermouth, lemon juice, rasberry syrup, and egg white in a cocktail shaker. **Dry-shake** the cocktail by shaking it without ice for 15 to 30 seconds to build the foam. **Fill** the shaker ¾ full with ice cubes and shake for about 12 seconds, or until chilled. **Strain** the cocktail into a coupe glass. **Garnish** with the raspberries on a cocktail pick.

Bramble

Tools: knife, jigger, citrus squeezer, shaker

The Bramble is a modern classic that brings together the refreshing and fruity flavors of gin, lemon, and blackberry. Although traditionally made with crème de mûre, a hard-to-find blackberry liqueur, it can also be made with homemade blackberry syrup.

2 ounces gin

1 ounce freshly squeezed lemon juice

½ ounce Simple Syrup (page 85)

½ ounce Berry Syrup (see page 159)

1 lemon slice, for garnish

1 blackberry, for garnish

Combine the gin, lemon juice, and simple syrup in a cocktail shaker. **Whip-shake** the cocktail by adding a few ice cubes to the cocktail shaker and shaking it until the cubes dissolve. **Fill** a rocks glass with crushed ice. **Pour** the cocktail into the glass. **Top** the glass with more crushed ice, and drizzle with the blackberry syrup. **Garnish** with the lemon slice and blackberry.

Hanky Panky

Tools: knife, jigger, mixing glass, bar spoon, strainer

The Hanky Panky is a classic gin cocktail that was created by famed bartender Ada Coleman in 1925. This simple blend of ingredients is a great introduction to the powerful and polarizing bitter liqueur Fernet Branca.

1½ ounces gin

1½ ounces sweet vermouth

2 dashes Fernet Branca

Orange twist, for garnish

Combine the gin, vermouth, and Fernet Branca in a mixing glass. **Fill** the mixing glass ¾ full with ice cubes and stir for about 30 seconds, or until chilled. **Strain** the cocktail into a coupe glass and garnish with an orange twist.

THE ESSENTIAL BAR BOOK FOR HOME MIXOLOGISTS

— 92 —

Famous Bartenders:
Ada Coleman

Ada Coleman, known as "Coley" to bar patrons and colleagues, was born in England in 1875. Perhaps one of the most famous female bartenders to date, she mixed her first cocktail in 1899 and worked her way up to a position as head bartender at the famous American Bar at the Savoy Hotel in London.

Coleman's enduring legacy is the delicious, classic gin cocktail, the Hanky Panky (page 92), invented for actor Charles Hawtrey. Other famous customers included Mark Twain, Charlie Chaplin, and Marlene Dietrich. By the end of her 20-plus-year stint behind the bar, Coley estimated she had served 100,000 customers and poured one million drinks.

GIN

Corpse Reviver #2

Tools: knife, jigger, citrus squeezer, shaker, strainer

One of the classic hangover-remedy cocktails, the Corpse Reviver #2 is a very easy-to-drink mix of gin, lemon, triple sec, and the aperitif wine Lillet Blanc. An absinthe rinse adds complexity and an additional layer of herbal flavor.

¼ ounce absinthe, for rinsing

¾ ounce gin

¾ ounce Lillet Blanc

¾ ounce triple sec

¾ ounce freshly squeezed lemon juice

Orange twist, for garnish

Put the absinthe in a coupe glass and swirl to coat the inside. **Discard** the absinthe. **Combine** the gin, Lillet Blanc, triple sec, and lemon juice in a cocktail shaker. **Fill** the shaker ¾ full with ice cubes and shake for about 12 seconds, or until chilled. **Strain** the cocktail into the absinthe-rinsed coupe glass, and garnish with an orange twist.

Ramos Gin Fizz

Tools: knife, jigger, citrus squeezer, shaker, strainer

The Ramos Gin Fizz is an iconic New Orleans cocktail with sky-high foam and bright citrus flavors. This light, creamy cocktail is surprisingly refreshing, making it an interesting brunch alternative to old standbys like mimosas or Bloody Marys (page 54).

2 ounces gin

¾ ounce Simple Syrup (page 85)

½ ounce light cream

½ ounce freshly squeezed lemon juice

½ ounce freshly squeezed lime juice

1 large egg white

3 dashes orange blossom water

Soda water

Orange twist, for garnish

Combine the gin, simple syrup, light cream, lemon juice, lime juice, egg white, and orange blossom water in a cocktail shaker. **Dry-shake** the liquid by shaking it without ice for at least 30 seconds to build the foam. **Fill** the shaker ¾ full with ice cubes and shake for about 12 seconds, or until chilled. **Strain** the liquid into your glass and carefully top with soda water. **Garnish** with an orange twist.

⊛ You can create even more voluminous foam by adding the coil from a Hawthorne strainer, if you have one, to your shaker before dry-shaking.

CHAPTER 8

Whiskey

The earliest origins of whiskey are murky, and it's hotly debated whether it first appeared in Ireland or Scotland. No matter who made it first, whiskey eventually made its way to America, where its popularity exploded and our national spirit, bourbon whiskey, was born. In 1964, the US Congress declared bourbon America's official distilled spirit.

Old Fashioned	**99**	Whiskey Smash	**105**
Manhattan	**100**	Gold Rush	**106**
Boulevardier	**101**	Old Pal	**107**
Mint Julep	**102**	Sazerac	**108**
Whiskey Sour	**104**	Toronto	**110**

IF YOU'RE A WHISKEY DRINKER...

If you're devoted to this brown liquor, you might be interested in having a few of these bottles on hand so you can easily mix classic whiskey cocktails like the Sazerac (page 108) and the Toronto (page 110).

ABSINTHE (SS TO SSS): a potent spirit made with a blend of botanicals, including wormwood, anise, and fennel

FERNET BRANCA (SS): a strongly flavored, herbal, bittersweet liqueur with a secret blend of 27 botanicals

PEYCHAUD'S BITTERS (S): a bright red cocktail flavoring made from a blend of gentian root, licorice root, fruits, and spices

RYE WHISKEY (S TO SSS): a whiskey distilled from a grain blend that must be at least 51 percent rye

Old Fashioned

Tools: knife, jigger, mixing glass, bar spoon, strainer

The Old Fashioned is the original cocktail. A touch of sweetener, bitters, and citrus oils open up the flavors of the whiskey, making a strong, balanced, and very satisfying cocktail. Traditionally this cocktail was made with a muddled sugar cube, but it's much more efficient today to replace the sugar with a quarter ounce of simple syrup.

2 ounces whiskey

¼ ounce Simple Syrup (page 85)

2 dashes Angostura bitters

Orange twist, for garnish

Combine the whiskey, simple syrup, and bitters in a mixing glass. **Fill** the mixing glass ¾ full with ice cubes and stir for about 30 seconds, or until chilled. **Fill** a rocks glass with ice, or use one large ice cube. **Strain** the cocktail into the glass and garnish with an orange twist.

WHISKEY

Manhattan

Tools: jigger, mixing glass, bar spoon, strainer

The Manhattan is a simple and spirit-forward, whiskey cocktail flavored with the herbal profile of sweet vermouth. It's unclear who invented this timeless classic, but a common tale claims it first appeared at a party thrown at the Manhattan Club in New York. This strong and slightly sweet cocktail makes for an excellent after-dinner cocktail.

2 ounces bourbon

1 ounce sweet vermouth

2 dashes Angostura bitters

Cocktail cherry, for garnish

Combine the whiskey, vermouth, and bitters in a mixing glass. **Fill** the mixing glass ¾ full with ice cubes and stir for about 30 seconds, or until chilled. **Strain** the cocktail into a coupe glass and garnish with a cocktail cherry.

Boulevardier

Tools: knife, jigger, mixing glass, bar spoon, strainer

The Boulevardier is similar to the classic Negroni cocktail, replacing gin with bourbon whiskey. The Boulevardier first appeared in 1927 in Harry MacElhone's book *Barflies and Cocktails*. Although this classic is typically served on the rocks, some prefer to serve it up, in a coupe glass.

1 ounce bourbon

1 ounce Campari

1 ounce sweet vermouth

Orange twist, for garnish

Combine the bourbon, Campari, and vermouth in a mixing glass. **Fill** the mixing glass ¾ full with ice cubes and stir for about 30 seconds, or until chilled. **Fill** a rocks glass with ice or use one large ice cube. **Strain** the cocktail into the glass, and garnish with an orange twist.

Batch it: Multiply the recipe by the number of drinks you need. Put the bourbon, Campari, vermouth, and ½ ounce water for each serving in a large pitcher. Stir to combine and chill in the refrigerator for at least a few hours prior to serving. Pour the cocktails into rocks glasses filled with ice and garnish with orange twists.

Mint Julep

Tools: muddler, jigger, bar spoon

Like a refreshing, minty Old Fashioned (page 99), the Mint Julep is a blend of bourbon, mint, and simple syrup over crushed ice. This classic cocktail originated in the American South, where it has become an iconic warm-weather staple and is as essential to the Kentucky Derby as fancy hats.

10 mint leaves

¼ ounce Simple Syrup (page 85)

2 ounces bourbon

Mint sprig, for garnish

Put the mint leaves and syrup in a rocks glass. **Using** a muddler, gently press on the leaves a few times to release the oils. **Add** the bourbon and then fill the glass with crushed ice. **Stir** several times to chill, then top the glass with more crushed ice. **Garnish** with a sprig of mint.

Whiskey vs. Bourbon vs. Scotch vs. Rye

Whisk(e)y: Whiskeys are distilled spirits made from fermented grains and aged in wooden barrels. *Whiskey*—with an *e*—refers to whiskeys from America and Ireland, while *whisky* is from Canada, Japan, or Scotland.

Bourbon: Bourbon is an American whiskey made with at least 51 percent corn and has a sweeter flavor than most other whiskeys.

Scotch: Scotch is either malt or grain whisky produced according to legal standards in Scotland. There are several categories, including single malt, single grain, and blended.

Rye: Rye is made with at least 51 percent rye and has a characteristic dry, spicy flavor. Rye whiskeys are common in America and Canada.

Whiskey Sour

Tools: knife, jigger, citrus squeezer, shaker, strainer

The Whiskey Sour is a classic cocktail dating back to the 1860s when it first appeared in Jerry Thomas's *How to Mix Drinks*. Although the original Whiskey Sour was made simply with whiskey, sugar, and lemon juice, the addition of an egg white for a smooth and creamy mouthfeel has become the most popular variation.

2 ounces bourbon or rye whiskey

¾ ounce Simple Syrup (page 85)

¾ ounce freshly squeezed lemon juice

1 large egg white

Cocktail cherry, for garnish

3 drops Angostura bitters, for garnish (optional)

Combine the whiskey, simple syrup, lemon juice, and egg white in a cocktail shaker. **Dry-shake** the cocktail by shaking without ice for 15 to 30 seconds to build the foam. **Fill** the shaker ¾ full with ice cubes and shake for about 12 seconds, or until chilled. **Strain** the cocktail into a coupe glass, and garnish with a cocktail cherry. **Garnish** with the bitters (if using) on the surface of the foam. **Draw** a continuous line through the dots with a toothpick for a decorative look.

☞ If you don't like the idea of raw egg in your cocktails, you can opt for pasteurized egg whites (use ½ ounce), or skip it altogether.

Whiskey Smash

Tools: knife, shaker, muddler, jigger, strainer

The Whiskey Smash is a vintage classic, first appearing in 1862. Like a combination of the Whiskey Sour (page 104) and the Mint Julep (page 102), this crisp cocktail is a blend of bourbon, lemon, and mint.

½ lemon, cut into wedges

10 mint leaves

¾ ounce Simple Syrup (page 85)

2 ounces bourbon

Mint sprig, for garnish

Put the lemon wedges in a cocktail shaker and muddle to release the juices and oils. **Add** the mint leaves and press on them with the muddler a few times. **Pour** the simple syrup and bourbon into the shaker and fill ¾ full with ice cubes. **Shake** for about 12 seconds, or until chilled. **Fill** a rocks glass with ice. **Strain** the cocktail into the glass, and garnish with a mint sprig.

Gold Rush

Tools: knife, jigger, citrus squeezer, shaker, strainer

The Gold Rush is a modern riff on the Whiskey Sour (page 104), replacing simple syrup with honey syrup. This deliciously simple mix of bourbon, honey, and lemon was invented by T. J. Siegel at New York City bar Milk & Honey.

2 ounces bourbon

¾ ounce Honey Syrup (page 75)

¾ ounce freshly squeezed lemon juice

Combine the bourbon, honey syrup, and lemon juice in a cocktail shaker. **Fill** the shaker ¾ full with ice cubes and shake for about 12 seconds, or until chilled. **Fill** a rocks glass with ice cubes. **Strain** the cocktail into the glass.

Old Pal

Tools: knife, jigger, mixing glass, bar spoon, strainer

The Old Pal is a less-sweet version of the classic Boulevardier (page 101), replacing sweet vermouth with dry vermouth. The Old Pal was invented at Harry's New York Bar in Paris and named for the owner's friend, journalist William "Sparrow" Robertson. Robertson reportedly called everyone he met his "old pal."

1 ounce rye whiskey

1 ounce Campari

1 ounce dry vermouth

Lemon twist, for garnish

Combine the rye, Campari, and vermouth in a mixing glass. **Fill** the mixing glass ¾ full with ice cubes and stir for about 30 seconds, or until chilled. **Fill** a rocks glass with ice or use one large ice cube. **Strain** the cocktail into the glass and garnish with a lemon twist.

Sazerac

Tools: knife, jigger, mixing glass, bar spoon, strainer

The Sazerac is a vintage New Orleans cocktail that was created by Antoine Peychaud, the inventor of the famous Peychaud's bitters. This variation on the Old Fashioned (page 99) was originally made with Cognac instead of whiskey. Cognac became unavailable during the late 1860s when phylloxera, a type of aphid, nearly destroyed European grape cultivation. During that period, the Cognac in Sazerac was replaced with rye whiskey, creating the Sazerac we enjoy today.

¼ ounce absinthe, for rinsing

2 ounces rye whiskey

¼ ounce Simple Syrup (page 85)

4 dashes Peychaud's bitters

Lemon twist, for garnish

Put the absinthe in a rocks glass and swirl to coat the inside. **Discard** the absinthe. **Combine** the whiskey, simple syrup, and bitters in a mixing glass. **Fill** the mixing glass ¾ full with ice cubes and stir for about 30 seconds, or until chilled. **Strain** the cocktail into the absinthe-rinsed rocks glass and garnish with a lemon twist.

The Green Fairy

Absinthe is a spirit with a reputation for making those who consume it hallucinate. It was the drink of choice for writers and artists in the late 1800s—nicknamed "the green fairy" because of its distinctive green color. Today, science questions whether or not absinthe ever actually had the power to cause hallucinations. Modern absinthe won't give you trippy psychoactive side effects, but it will add an herbal, licorice-like flavor to a variety of cocktail recipes.

Toronto

Tools: knife, jigger, mixing glass, bar spoon, strainer

The Toronto is a variation on the Old Fashioned (page 99) that combines spicy rye whiskey with a touch of the bittersweet liqueur Fernet Branca. This simple cocktail showcases the flavor of the whiskey against a backdrop of herbaceous, complex, and minty Fernet.

2 ounces rye whiskey

¼ ounce Simple Syrup (page 85)

¼ ounce Fernet Branca

2 dashes Angostura bitters

Orange twist, for garnish

Combine the rye, simple syrup, Fernet Branca, and bitters in a mixing glass. **Fill** the mixing glass ¾ full with ice cubes and stir for about 30 seconds, or until chilled. **Strain** the cocktail into a coupe glass and garnish with an orange twist.

CHAPTER 9

Tequila

The first agave spirits were made in the 16th century when Spanish conquistadors brought their knowledge of distillation to Mexico. Those early distilled spirits would eventually become the tequila we know today. Though there aren't as many classic cocktails that use tequila as some other liquors, few cocktails have garnered the tremendous global popularity of the beloved Margarita.

Paloma **115**	Tequila Sunrise **121**
Margarita **116**	Oaxacan Old Fashioned . . . **122**
Tommy's Margarita. **118**	El Diablo **124**
Cantarito **120**	Silk Stocking **125**

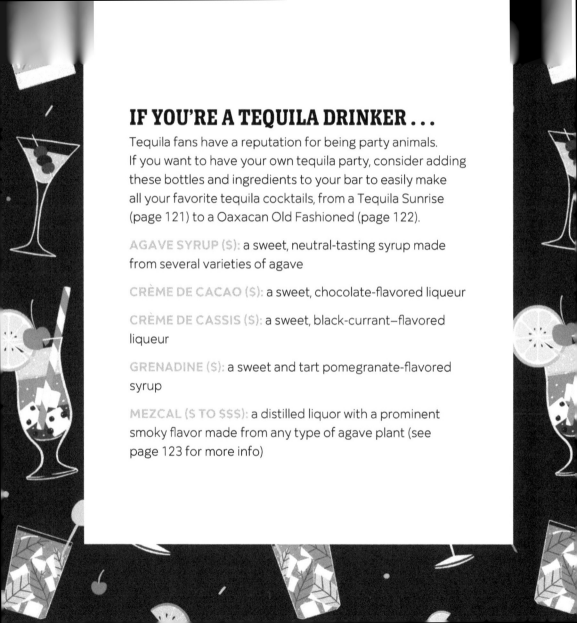

IF YOU'RE A TEQUILA DRINKER . . .

Tequila fans have a reputation for being party animals. If you want to have your own tequila party, consider adding these bottles and ingredients to your bar to easily make all your favorite tequila cocktails, from a Tequila Sunrise (page 121) to a Oaxacan Old Fashioned (page 122).

AGAVE SYRUP ($): a sweet, neutral-tasting syrup made from several varieties of agave

CRÈME DE CACAO ($): a sweet, chocolate-flavored liqueur

CRÈME DE CASSIS ($): a sweet, black-currant–flavored liqueur

GRENADINE ($): a sweet and tart pomegranate-flavored syrup

MEZCAL ($ TO $$$): a distilled liquor with a prominent smoky flavor made from any type of agave plant (see page 123 for more info)

Paloma

Tools: knife, jigger, citrus squeezer, bar spoon

The simple and delicious Paloma is often referred to as Mexico's most popular cocktail. This easy, three-ingredient cocktail can be made with either tequila or smoky mezcal and topped with grapefruit soda or a combination of fresh grapefruit juice, simple syrup, and soda water.

2 ounces tequila

½ ounce freshly squeezed lime juice

6 ounces grapefruit soda, chilled

Lime slice, for garnish

Fill a highball glass with ice cubes. **Pour** the tequila and lime juice into the glass and stir several times to chill. **Fill** the glass with the grapefruit soda and garnish with a lime slice.

If you aren't able to find grapefruit soda, you can also use a combination of 2 ounces fresh grapefruit juice and ½ ounce Simple Syrup (page 85), topped with soda water.

Margarita

Tools: knife, jigger, citrus squeezer, shaker, strainer

The Margarita is the quintessential tequila cocktail, and one of the most popular cocktails in the world. There are many stories regarding the origin of the Margarita, but it's unclear who first created this sublime mix of tequila, orange liqueur, and fresh lime juice. Although this classic recipe calls for the drink to be served on the rocks, the Margarita can also be served up in a coupe glass, or frozen, blended with a cup of crushed ice—the tip on the next page will show you how.

Lime wedge, for garnish

Coarse salt, for the rim (optional)

2 ounces tequila

1 ounce triple sec

1 ounce freshly squeezed lime juice

¼ ounce Simple Syrup (optional)

If you prefer a salted rim: **Run** the lime wedge along half of the outside rim of a rocks glass. **Fill** a shallow dish with the coarse salt and dip that rim in the dish. **Shake** the glass gently to remove any excess. **Combine** the tequila, triple sec, lime juice, and simple syrup (if using) in a cocktail shaker. **Fill** the shaker ¾ full with ice cubes and shake for about 12 seconds, or until chilled. **Strain** the cocktail into the glass and garnish with the lime wedge.

⊗ A classic Margarita can be made with just tequila, triple sec, and lime juice. However, some prefer the addition of ¼ ounce of simple syrup for slightly more sweetness. Try it both ways and see which you prefer.

⊗ Make it a frozen Margarita by combining all ingredients with 1 cup of ice in a blender. Blend on high until smooth, then pour the cocktail into your glass and garnish with a lime wedge.

Tommy's Margarita

Tools: knife, jigger, citrus squeezer, shaker, strainer

Tommy's Margarita is a simple Margarita variation made with tequila, fresh lime juice, and agave syrup. This wildly popular cocktail was invented by Julio Bermejo in the 1990s at Tommy's Mexican Restaurant in San Francisco.

2 ounces tequila

1 ounce freshly squeezed lime juice

½ ounce agave syrup

Lime wedge, for garnish

Combine the tequila, lime juice, and agave syrup in a cocktail shaker. **Fill** the shaker ¾ full with ice cubes and shake for about 12 seconds, or until chilled. **Strain** the cocktail into a rocks glass and garnish with a lime wedge.

Batch it: Multiply the recipe by the number of drinks you need. In a large pitcher, combine the tequila, fresh lime juice, agave syrup, and ½ ounce water for each drink and stir several times to combine. Chill for at least a few hours. Pour the cocktail into rocks glasses filled with ice and garnish with lime wedges. If you have an immersion blender, quickly blend the margaritas in the pitcher just before serving. This mimics shaking, creating a better texture.

Famous Fictional Bars

Sharing a drink with pals at the local watering hole is a tradition that expands even into fictional worlds. Here are some bars where your favorite characters go to drink.

CHEERS: a place where everybody knows your name, and Sam Malone will pour you a drink

MOE'S TAVERN: the bar where Homer Simpson spends most of his time saddled up

PADDY'S PUB: the bar from *It's Always Sunny in Philadelphia* where the gang begins every misadventure

MOS EISLEY CANTINA: a Star Wars dive bar on planet Tatooine where fights tend to break out

THE LEAKY CAULDRON: a pub in the Harry Potter universe where wizards wet their whistles

TEQUILA

Cantarito

Tools: knife, jigger, citrus squeezer, shaker, strainer

The Cantarito is a very popular cocktail in Mexico that resembles a Paloma (page 115) with additional citrus juices and a pinch of salt. The Cantarito gets its name from the small clay pot it's traditionally served in, which is called a *cántaro*.

2 ounces tequila

½ ounce freshly squeezed grapefruit juice

½ ounce freshly squeezed orange juice

½ ounce freshly squeezed lime juice

Pinch salt

3 ounces grapefruit soda

Citrus slices, for garnish

Combine the tequila, grapefruit juice, orange juice, lime juice, and salt in a cocktail shaker. **Fill** the shaker ¾ full with ice cubes and shake for about 12 seconds, or until chilled. **Fill** a highball glass with ice cubes. **Strain** the liquid into the glass and top with the grapefruit soda. **Garnish** with slices of lime, grapefruit, or orange.

Tequila Sunrise

Tools: knife, jigger, citrus squeezer, bar spoon

The classic Tequila Sunrise is made with tequila, orange juice, and a bit of grenadine. This mix can lean a bit too sweet, so I like to add ½ ounce of fresh lime juice to balance things out. Be sure to use freshly squeezed orange juice for best results.

1½ ounces tequila

4 ounces freshly squeezed orange juice

½ ounce freshly squeezed lime juice

¼ ounce grenadine

Orange slice, for garnish

Cocktail cherry, for garnish

Fill a highball glass with ice. **Pour** the tequila, orange juice, and lime juice into the glass and stir several times to chill. **Pour** in the grenadine slowly, allowing it to sink to the bottom. **Garnish** with an orange slice and a cocktail cherry. **Serve** with a straw and stir before drinking.

Oaxacan Old Fashioned

Tools: knife, jigger, mixing glass, bar spoon, strainer

The Oaxacan Old Fashioned was created by bartender Phil Ward in New York City in 2007. Using a split base of tequila and mezcal, it's a wonderful cocktail for getting to know the finer flavors of agave spirits.

1½ ounces tequila

½ ounce mezcal

¼ ounce agave syrup

2 dashes Angostura bitters

Flamed orange twist, for garnish (see technique on page 29)

Combine the tequila, mezcal, agave syrup, and bitters in a mixing glass. **Fill** the mixing glass ¾ full with ice cubes and stir for about 12 seconds, or until chilled. **Fill** a rocks glass with ice or use one large ice cube. **Strain** the cocktail into the glass filled with ice (or over one large cube), and garnish with a flamed orange twist.

Mezcal, a Primer

Mezcal is a distinctively smoky spirit imported from Mexico, primarily the Oaxaca region. In order for a spirit to be considered mezcal, it has to meet a certain set of government-mandated requirements, which meant that for a long time, it was hard to find in America (but thankfully that is not the case anymore!).

During the distillation process, the hearts of the agave plants, known as *piñas*, are cooked in underground pits, which is what gives the liquor its characteristic campfire flavor.

Fun fact: Tequila is actually a type of mezcal made with uncooked piñas of the blue agave plant.

TEQUILA

El Diablo

Tools: knife, jigger, citrus squeezer, shaker, strainer

The El Diablo is thought to have been invented by famed tiki cocktail creator Victor "Trader Vic" Bergeron in the 1940s. The combination of fruity black currant liqueur, lime juice, and spicy ginger beer pairs perfectly with tequila in this refreshing cocktail.

2 ounces tequila

¾ ounce freshly squeezed lime juice

½ ounce crème de cassis

4 ounces ginger beer

Lime wedge, for garnish

Combine the tequila, lime juice, and crème de cassis in a cocktail shaker. **Fill** the shaker ¾ full with ice cubes and shake for about 12 seconds, or until chilled. **Fill** a highball glass with ice cubes. **Strain** the liquid into the glass and top with the ginger beer. **Garnish** with a lime wedge.

Silk Stocking

Tools: jigger, shaker, strainer

The Silk Stocking is an unusual tequila-based dessert cocktail. This smooth and creamy pale pink drink features flavors of agave, chocolate, and a hint of fruity pomegranate.

2 ounces tequila

1 ounce crème de cacao

1 ounce cream

¼ ounce grenadine

Ground cinnamon, for garnish

Combine the tequila, crème de cacao, cream, and grenadine in a cocktail shaker. **Fill** the shaker ¾ full with ice cubes and shake for about 12 seconds, or until chilled. **Strain** the cocktail into your glass and garnish with a sprinkle of cinnamon.

CHAPTER 10

Brandy

Brandy is a key ingredient in some of the oldest classic cocktail recipes. Made from fermented fruit juice, brandies like Cognac add a smooth, rich sweetness to cocktails like the Sidecar and the Brandy Alexander.

Sidecar	**129**	Corpse Reviver #1	**134**
Brandy Old Fashioned	**130**	Japanese Cocktail	**135**
Brandy Alexander	**131**	Fish House Punch	**136**
Scorpion	**132**	Fish House Punch for a Bunch	**137**

IF YOU'RE A BRANDY DRINKER . . .

There's just something classy about brandy. If you're a fan, these additional spirits will give your bar the power to make all the best brandy cocktails, like Fish House Punch (page 136) or a Scorpion (page 132).

AGED RUM ($ TO $$$): rum that's been barrel aged for at least three years

CALVADOS ($$ TO $$$): a type of brandy made from apples in the Normandy region of France

CRÈME DE CACAO ($): a sweet, chocolate-flavored liqueur

ORGEAT ($): a syrup made with almonds and a touch of orange blossom water

PEACH LIQUEUR ($): a peach-flavored liqueur

Sidecar

Tools: knife, jigger, citrus squeezer, shaker, strainer

The Sidecar is one of the best-known brandy cocktails. This simple mix of Cognac, orange liqueur, and lemon juice dates back to the early 1920s. By the 1930s, a sugared rim was added to the recipe, offsetting the tartness of the drink.

Lemon wedge, for the rim

Sugar, for the rim

2 ounces Cognac

1 ounce triple sec

¾ ounce freshly squeezed lemon juice

Lemon twist, for garnish

Rub a lemon wedge along the rim of a coupe glass. **Fill** a shallow dish with sugar and carefully dip the rim of the glass, keeping the sugar on the outside rim. **Shake** to remove any excess. **Combine** the Cognac, triple sec, and lemon juice in a cocktail shaker. **Fill** the shaker ¾ full with ice cubes and shake for about 12 seconds, or until chilled. **Strain** the cocktail into the sugar-rimmed coupe glass and garnish with a lemon twist.

BRANDY

Brandy Old Fashioned

Tools: knife, jigger, mixing glass, bar spoon, strainer

If you enjoy simple, spirit-forward cocktails like the whiskey Old Fashioned (page 99), try it with brandy. This cocktail is an excellent way to get to know the more subtle flavors in fine spirits. I like to garnish this drink with both an orange twist and a cocktail cherry to underscore the naturally sweet, dried-fruit flavors of the liquor.

2 ounces brandy
or Cognac

¼ ounce Simple Syrup
(page 85)

2 dashes Angostura
bitters

Orange twist, for garnish

Cocktail cherry, for
garnish

Combine the brandy, simple syrup, and bitters in a mixing glass. **Fill** the mixing glass ¾ full with ice cubes and stir for about 30 seconds, or until chilled. **Fill** a rocks glass with ice. **Strain** the cocktail into the glass filled with ice and garnish with an orange twist and a cocktail cherry.

Brandy Alexander

Tools: jigger, shaker, strainer, grater

This decadent dessert cocktail features smooth Cognac with rich chocolate liqueur and cream. Originally created with gin, the brandy version has far surpassed the original in popularity. Don't skip the finishing touch of freshly grated nutmeg, as the aromatics add another dimension of flavor.

1½ ounces Cognac

1 ounce crème de cacao

1 ounce cream

Freshly grated nutmeg, for garnish

Combine the Cognac, crème de cacao, and cream in a cocktail shaker. **Fill** the shaker ¾ full with ice cubes and shake for about 12 seconds, or until chilled. **Strain** the cocktail into your glass and garnish with freshly grated nutmeg.

Scorpion

Tools: knife, jigger, citrus squeezer, blender

The Scorpion is one of the best-known tiki cocktails, often served in a large format to groups and called a Scorpion Bowl. The story goes that legendary tiki cocktail inventor Victor "Trader Vic" Bergeron was inspired by a similar bowl-style cocktail he saw at a bar in Honolulu. Bergeron brought the concept back to his restaurant in California and created his own infamous interpretation with rum and brandy.

1 ounce Cognac

1 ounce aged rum

2 ounces freshly squeezed orange juice

1 ounce freshly squeezed lemon juice

½ ounce orgeat

Orange slice, for garnish

Mint sprig, for garnish

Combine the Cognac, rum, orange juice, lemon juice, and orgeat in a blender. **Add** 1 cup of crushed ice to the blender and blend on high speed until smooth. **Pour** the cocktail into a highball glass and garnish with an orange slice and a sprig of mint.

Famous Bartenders:
Trader Vic

Not to be confused with grocery superstar Trader Joe, "Trader Vic" (Victor Jules Bergeron, Jr.) was born in San Francisco on December 10, 1902. He opened his first restaurant, Hinky Dinks, in Oakland in 1934, but inspired by the success of Don the Beachcomber (and convinced he could do better), he switched tack and rebranded as the tiki-themed Trader Vic's.

Though there is some debate, Trader Vic is considered to be the creator of the Mai Tai (page 77) as we know it today, as well as other now-classic tropical drinks, including the Scorpion (page 132).

Corpse Reviver #1

Tools: jigger, mixing glass, bar spoon, strainer

Corpse Revivers are a family of cocktails dating back to the 1800s that were intended to cure hangovers. In the classic *The Savoy Cocktail Book*, Harry Craddock notes of the Corpse Reviver #1, "To be taken before 11 a.m., or anytime steam or energy is needed." I personally can't imagine drinking a Corpse Reviver #1 in the morning, but it does make for a lovely, Manhattan-style after-dinner drink.

1 ounce Cognac

1 ounce Calvados

½ ounce sweet vermouth

Combine the Cognac, Calvados, and vermouth in a mixing glass. **Fill** the mixing glass ¾ full with ice cubes and stir for about 30 seconds, or until chilled. **Strain** the cocktail into a coupe glass.

Japanese Cocktail

Tools: knife, jigger, shaker, strainer

The Japanese Cocktail is a classic almond-flavored Cognac cocktail dating back to the late 1800s. The drink first appeared in the bar book *How to Mix Drinks* by Jerry Thomas, but it's unclear how the drink made with French brandy came to acquire its name.

2 ounces Cognac

½ ounce orgeat

2 dashes Angostura bitters

Lemon twist, for garnish

Combine the Cognac, orgeat, and bitters in a cocktail shaker. **Fill** the shaker ¾ full with ice cubes and shake for about 12 seconds, or until chilled. **Strain** the cocktail into a coupe glass and garnish with a lemon twist.

BRANDY

Fish House Punch

Tools: knife, jigger, citrus squeezer, shaker, strainer, grater

This classic punch recipe originated at a social club in Pennsylvania some-time before 1800. The blend of Cognac, aged rum, peach, and lemon is rich, balanced, and slightly fruity, making it an ideal batched cocktail for parties.

1 ounce Cognac

1 ounce aged rum

¾ ounce peach liqueur

1 ounce freshly squeezed lemon juice

½ ounce Simple Syrup (page 85)

2 ounces black tea, chilled

Lemon wheel, for garnish

Freshly grated nutmeg, for garnish

Combine the Cognac, rum, liqueur, lemon juice, and simple syrup in a cocktail shaker. **Fill** the shaker ¾ full with ice and shake for about 12 seconds, or until chilled. **Fill** a highball glass with ice. **Strain** the liquid into the glass filled with ice and top with the tea. **Garnish** with a lemon wheel and freshly grated nutmeg.

🍶 Cold black tea is the most common lengthener used to add dilution to this cocktail, but you can substitute sparkling water for a fizzy punch.

Fish House Punch for a Bunch

Tools: knife, jigger, citrus squeezer, mixing bowl, measuring cups, ladle

One of my favorite large-format cocktails, this punch is a big step up from any sweet, brightly colored concoctions.

1½ cups Cognac

1½ cups aged rum

1 cup peach liqueur

1½ cups freshly squeezed lemon juice (about 12 lemons)

¾ to 1 cup Simple Syrup (page 85)

2 to 3 cups chilled black tea

Lemon wheel, for garnish

Freshly grated nutmeg, for garnish

Freeze a large metal mixing bowl or Bundt pan filled with water the night before the punch is needed. To serve: **Remove** the ice block from the freezer, and place it in a punch bowl. **Pour** the Cognac, rum, liqueur, lemon juice, and simple syrup over the ice. **Stir** in the tea (or substitute sparkling water) to taste. **Ladle** the punch into glasses filled with ice and garnish each with a lemon wheel and freshly grated nutmeg. *Serves 10*

CHAPTER 11

Champagne & Sparkling Wines

Champagne and sparkling wines are the definitive drinks of celebrations, big and small. These nine bubbly cocktails will liven up any event, from Sunday brunch to a wedding reception or just a casual, weekday happy hour.

Champagne Cocktail **141**

French 75 . . . . **142**

Negroni Sbagliato **143**

Champagne Margarita. **145**

Aperol Spritz. **146**

Old Cuban **147**

Seelbach. **148**

Airmail **149**

Death in the Afternoon **151**

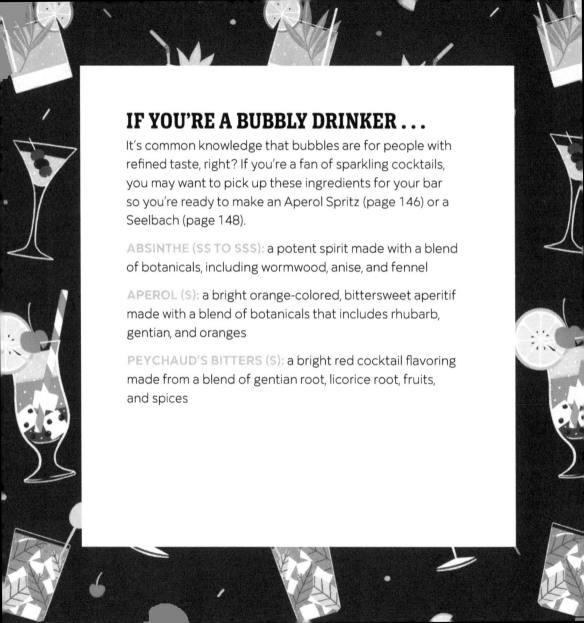

IF YOU'RE A BUBBLY DRINKER . . .

It's common knowledge that bubbles are for people with refined taste, right? If you're a fan of sparkling cocktails, you may want to pick up these ingredients for your bar so you're ready to make an Aperol Spritz (page 146) or a Seelbach (page 148).

ABSINTHE ($$ TO $$$): a potent spirit made with a blend of botanicals, including wormwood, anise, and fennel

APEROL ($): a bright orange-colored, bittersweet aperitif made with a blend of botanicals that includes rhubarb, gentian, and oranges

PEYCHAUD'S BITTERS ($): a bright red cocktail flavoring made from a blend of gentian root, licorice root, fruits, and spices

Champagne Cocktail

Tools: knife, jigger

The Champagne Cocktail is thought to be one of the oldest cocktails, created sometime in the 1800s before the first cocktail recipe books were published. The timeless mix of bitters, sugar, and Champagne is the sparkling wine equivalent of the whiskey Old Fashioned (page 99).

2 dashes
Angostura bitters

1 sugar cube

4 ounces Champagne, chilled

Lemon twist, for garnish

Drop the bitters onto the sugar cube and put the sugar cube in a Champagne flute. **Pour** the Champagne into the glass and garnish with a lemon twist.

French 75

Tools: knife, jigger, citrus squeezer, shaker, strainer

The French 75 is an easy-to-drink but potent gin and Champagne cocktail that's brightened with fresh lemon juice and a splash of simple syrup. Named for the French 75-mm field gun, this cocktail packs a punch.

1½ ounces gin

¾ ounce freshly squeezed lemon juice

¾ ounce Simple Syrup (page 85)

3 ounces Champagne, chilled

Lemon twist, for garnish

Combine the gin, lemon juice, and simple syrup in a cocktail shaker. **Fill** the shaker ¾ full with ice cubes and shake for about 12 seconds, or until chilled. **Strain** the liquid into a Champagne flute and top with the Champagne. **Garnish** with a lemon twist.

Batch it: Multiply the recipe by the number of drinks. Chill your bottles overnight. On the day itself, juice enough lemons for ¾ ounce fresh juice per drink (see page 20). In a large pitcher, pour in the gin, simple syrup, and lemon juice and stir. Refrigerate until needed. To serve, add 3 ounces to each glass, top with Champagne, and garnish with lemon twists.

Negroni Sbagliato

Tools: knife, jigger, mixing glass, bar spoon, strainer

The Negroni Sbagliato is a sparkling variation of the classic Negroni. *Sbagliato* is Italian for "mistaken," and according to legend, this cocktail was created when a bartender mistakenly added prosecco to a Negroni instead of gin.

1 ounce Campari

1 ounce sweet vermouth

1 ounce prosecco or other dry sparkling wine

Orange twist, for garnish

Combine the Campari and sweet vermouth in a mixing glass. **Fill** the mixing glass ¾ full with ice cubes and stir for about 30 seconds, or until chilled. **Fill** a rocks glass with ice. **Strain** the liquid into the glass and top with the prosecco. **Garnish** with an orange twist.

Songs about Drinking

Alcohol has been the muse of musicians since the beginning of time. Here are a few *intoxicating* songs to add to your party playlist.

"Margaritaville" by Jimmy Buffett

"Tequila" by The Champs

"Drunk in Love" by Beyoncé

"Escape (The Piña Colada Song)" by Rupert Holmes

"Whiskey River" by Johnny Bush

"Gin & Juice" by Snoop Dogg

"Tubthumping" by Chumbawamba

"Tipsy" by J-Kwon

"Red Red Wine" by UB40

"Shots" by LMFAO

"There's a Tear in My Beer" by Hank Williams

"Rum and Coca-Cola" by The Andrews Sisters

Champagne Margarita

Tools: knife, jigger, citrus squeezer, shaker, strainer

This sparkling margarita is a crowd-pleaser that's fun and easy to batch for parties. The Champagne Margarita combines tequila, orange liqueur, lime juice, and a few ounces of bubbly for a wonderful celebratory cocktail any time of year.

1 ounce tequila

¾ ounce triple sec

¾ ounce freshly squeezed lime juice

3 ounces Champagne, chilled

Lime wheel, for garnish

Combine the tequila, triple sec, and lime juice in a cocktail shaker. **Fill** the shaker ¾ full with ice cubes and shake for about 12 seconds, or until chilled. **Strain** the liquid into a Champagne flute and top with the Champagne. **Garnish** with a lime wheel.

Batch it: Multiply the recipe by the number of drinks you need. Put the tequila, triple sec, and fresh lime juice in a large pitcher and stir several times to combine. Chill for at least a few hours before serving. Shortly before the party, set out glasses and pour 2½ ounces of the mix in each. As guests arrive, top each glass with chilled Champagne and garnish.

Aperol Spritz

Tools: knife, jigger, bar spoon

Although this classic Italian spritz first became popular in the 1950s, it has exploded in popularity around the world in recent years. Light, gently bittersweet, and low-ABV, the Aperol Spritz is the quintessential cocktail for aperitivo.

2 ounces Aperol

3 ounces prosecco

1 ounce soda water

Orange slice, for garnish

Fill your glass with ice cubes. **Add** the Aperol and top with the prosecco and soda water. **Stir** gently to combine, and garnish with an orange slice.

Old Cuban

Tools: knife, jigger, citrus squeezer, shaker, strainer

The Old Cuban was invented by Audrey Saunders at the Pegu Club in 2001. This fresh and bubbly cocktail drinks like a combination of a French 75 and a Mojito, with rum, lime, mint, and sparkling wine.

1½ ounces aged rum

¾ ounce freshly squeezed lime juice

¾ ounce Simple Syrup (page 85)

6 mint leaves

2 dashes Angostura bitters

2 ounces Champagne or other dry sparkling wine

Mint sprig, for garnish

Combine the rum, lime juice, simple syrup, mint leaves, and bitters in a cocktail shaker. **Fill** the shaker ¾ full with ice cubes and shake for about 12 seconds, or until chilled. **Strain** the liquid into a coupe glass and top with the Champagne. **Garnish** with a sprig of mint.

Seelbach

Tools: knife, jigger, mixing glass, bar spoon

The Seelbach is a unique Champagne cocktail that's fortified with bourbon, flavored with a touch of orange liqueur, and seasoned with a heavy dose of bitters. Originally thought to be a rediscovered vintage cocktail of the Seelbach Hotel in Louisville, Kentucky, it was revealed in recent years that the drink was actually created in the 1990s.

1 ounce bourbon

½ ounce triple sec

7 dashes Angostura bitters

7 dashes Peychaud's bitters

4 ounces Champagne or other dry sparkling wine, chilled

Orange twist, for garnish

Combine the bourbon, triple sec, Angostura bitters, and Peychaud's bitters in a mixing glass. **Fill** the mixing glass ¾ full with ice cubes and stir for about 30 seconds, or until chilled. **Strain** the liquid into a Champagne flute and top with the Champagne. **Garnish** with an orange twist.

Airmail

Tools: knife, jigger, citrus squeezer, shaker, strainer

The Airmail cocktail first appeared in the 1930s, not long after Airmail service first began in Cuba. Originally made with then-Cuban Bacardi rum, honey, lime, and Champagne, the Airmail drinks like a luscious, tropical French 75.

1½ ounces aged rum

¾ ounce freshly squeezed lime juice

¾ ounce Honey Syrup (page 75)

3 ounces Champagne, chilled

Lime twist, for garnish

Combine the rum, lime juice, and honey syrup in a cocktail shaker. **Fill** the shaker ¾ full with ice cubes and shake for about 12 seconds, or until chilled. **Fill** a highball glass with ice. **Strain** the liquid into the glass and top with the Champagne. **Garnish** with a lime twist.

Books about Drinking

DRINK: A Cultural History of Alcohol by Iain Gately
A thorough and fascinating guide to the history of booze, this book is filled with stories of how spirits and alcoholic beverages originated and became part of cultures around the world.

The Drunken Botanist by Amy Stewart
In this exploration of the botanicals behind the booze, Stewart explains how humankind has found ways to transform plants into intoxicating brews throughout history and includes some classic cocktail recipes, too.

IMBIBE! by David Wondrich
A prominent cocktail historian, Wondrich has helped uncover the murky histories of some of the world's great cocktails. *IMBIBE!* is an in-depth and entertaining look at classic American cocktails.

On Booze by F. Scott Fitzgerald
On Booze is an intoxicating collection of alcohol-related F. Scott Fitzgerald short stories.

Death in the Afternoon

Tools: jigger

Famed author Ernest Hemingway is said to have created this powerful cocktail and named it after one of his novels. Hemingway's instructions for this cocktail included consuming three to five of them slowly, but given the high alcohol content, I'd recommend enjoying just one at a time!

1 ounce absinthe

3 ounces Champagne or other dry sparkling wine, chilled

Pour the absinthe into a Champagne flute. **Top** with the Champagne.

🍃 For the best-tasting cocktail, chill your absinthe in the freezer before pouring.

CHAPTER 12

Mocktails

Sometimes you want a well-crafted drink without the alcohol. This chapter features six delicious mocktail recipes, from the classic Virgin Piña Colada to a spicy, nonalcoholic Moscow Mule.

Virgin Piña Colada **155**

Spicy Mock-scow Mule **156**

Earl Grey Cobbler **157**

Strawberry-Lavender Soda . **158**

Berry Syrup. **159**

Ginger Limeade. **160**

Virgin Floradora. **162**

IF YOU'RE NOT A DRINKER . . .

Mocktails can be made with just as much care and layering of flavors as alcoholic drinks. Consider adding these accessories and ingredients to your bar to give booze-free drinks some extra flair.

COPPER MULE MUGS: If you like to mix up mock Mules, invest in a couple of copper mugs to keep your drinks extra frosty.

FANCY STRAWS: Reusable metal straws are a fun (and eco-friendly) addition to the home bar and make drinks even more enjoyable.

EDIBLE FLOWERS: Edible flowers like orchids or lavender make for the perfect garnish for mocktails like the Virgin Piña Colada (page 155) or Strawberry-Lavender Soda (page 158).

Virgin Piña Colada

Tools: knife, jigger, citrus squeezer, blender

This nonalcoholic Piña Colada is just as delicious as its boozier counterpart. The flavors of pineapple, coconut, and lime are blended with a cup of crushed ice for a smooth, frozen tropical treat.

3 ounces pineapple juice

1 ounce cream of coconut

¾ ounce freshly squeezed lime juice

Pineapple wedge, for garnish

Cocktail cherry, for garnish

Put the pineapple juice, cream of coconut, and lime juice in a blender. **Add** 1 cup of crushed ice and blend on high speed until smooth. **Pour** the drink into your glass and garnish with a pineapple wedge and a cocktail cherry.

Spicy Mock-scow Mule

Tools: knife, jigger, citrus squeezer, muddler, bar spoon

Even if you're not imbibing, you can still enjoy the flavor of a spicy Moscow Mule. For a milder version, skip the muddled jalapeño.

1 to 2 thin jalapeño pepper slices

¾ ounce freshly squeezed lime juice

6 ounces ginger beer

Lime wedge, for garnish

Muddle the jalapeño with the lime juice in your glass. **Fill** the glass with ice cubes and top with the ginger beer. **Stir** gently and garnish with a lime wedge.

⊘ I recommend using a quality ginger beer such as Fever-Tree or Q Mixers. For a fruitier variation, try Reed's ginger beer. It's a Jamaican-style ginger beer made with honey and pineapple.

Earl Grey Cobbler

Tools: knife, jigger, muddler, shaker, strainer

This mocktail variation of the classic Sherry Cobbler uses chilled Earl Grey tea in place of fortified wine. A small amount of sweetener and some muddled citrus brighten the flavor of the tea and make for a very refreshing afternoon sipper.

3 thin orange slices

¼ ounce Simple Syrup (page 85)

3 ounces Earl Grey tea, chilled

Berries or seasonal fruit, for garnish

Mint sprig, for garnish

Muddle the orange slices with the simple syrup in a cocktail shaker. **Add** the tea to the shaker, fill ¾ full with ice cubes and shake for about 12 seconds, or until chilled. **Fill** your glass with crushed ice. **Strain** the drink into the glass and garnish with a sprig of mint and berries.

Strawberry-Lavender Soda

Tools: knife, strainer, jigger

This simple, fresh and floral mocktail is made with a delicious homemade syrup that takes just minutes to make.

For the strawberry-lavender syrup

1 cup sugar

1 cup water

2 cups strawberries, chopped

1 to 2 tablespoons dried culinary-grade lavender

For the drink

1 ounce strawberry-lavender syrup

6 ounces soda water

Lemon wedge

To make the strawberry-lavender syrup

Put the sugar and water in a small saucepan and heat over medium heat, stirring frequently, until the sugar has dissolved. **Add** the strawberries and bring to a boil. **Reduce** the heat to low and simmer for 5 minutes, or until the fruit begins to break down. **Remove** from the heat. **Add** the lavender and stir to incorporate. **Cover** the saucepan and allow the syrup to cool fully before straining out the strawberries and lavender. **Store** the syrup in a sealed glass container in the refrigerator for up to two weeks.

To make the drink

Fill a highball glass with ice cubes. **Pour** the syrup over the ice and top with the soda water. **Squeeze** the lemon wedge over the drink and drop it in.

Berry Syrup

Berry syrup adds a bright, berry flavor to classic cocktails like the Clover Club (page 90) and Bramble (page 91). Use the type of berries the recipes in the book call for, or go rogue and experiment with what you have on hand. Store the syrup in a sealable container in the refrigerator for up to two weeks.

1 cup water

1 cup sugar

2 cups berries, such as raspberries or blackberries

Combine the water and sugar in a small saucepan. **Heat** the water and sugar over medium heat and stir frequently until the sugar has dissolved. **Bring** to a boil and add the berries. **Reduce** the heat to low and simmer for 5 to 10 minutes, or just until the fruit begins to break down. **Remove** from the heat and allow the syrup to cool for about 30 minutes. **Strain** out the berries, once cool, using a fine-mesh strainer, and discard. *Makes about 2 cups*

Ginger Limeade

Tools: knife, jigger, citrus squeezer, shaker, strainer

This refreshing and slightly spicy Ginger Limeade is a great alcohol-free drink to batch on hot summer days. Bonus: Ginger can help settle the stomach, so I like to mix this with sparkling water for occasional stomach upsets. Use ¼ cup chopped ginger for a milder syrup, ½ cup for a spicier syrup.

For the ginger syrup

1 cup water

1 cup sugar

¼ to ½ cup chopped, peeled fresh ginger

For the drink

1 ounce freshly squeezed lime juice

1 ounce ginger syrup

4 ounces cold water

Lime slice, for garnish

To make the ginger syrup

Combine the water and sugar in a small saucepan over medium heat, stirring frequently, until the sugar has dissolved. **Add** the ginger and bring to a boil. **Reduce** the heat to low and simmer for 10 minutes. **Remove** from the heat and allow to cool fully before straining out the ginger. **Store** the ginger syrup in a sealed glass container in the refrigerator for up to two weeks.

To make the drink

Combine the lime juice, ginger syrup, and water in a cocktail shaker. **Fill** the shaker ¾ full with ice cubes and shake for about 12 seconds, or until chilled. **Fill** a highball glass with ice. **Strain** the drink into the glass and garnish with a lime slice.

⊘ If you prefer a sparkling limeade, shake the lime juice, syrup, and 1 ounce of water until chilled. Strain into the ice-filled glass, then top with 3 ounces of soda water.

Batch it: Combine 1 cup freshly squeezed lime juice (see page 20 for estimating how many limes you'll need) with 1 cup ginger syrup in a large pitcher. Add 4 to 5 cups cold water and stir several times to combine. Serve in highball glasses filled with ice cubes and garnish each with a lime slice.

Virgin Floradora

Tools: knife, jigger, citrus squeezer, bar spoon

The Floradora is a classic gin cocktail, but its nonalcoholic ingredients make a delicious mocktail as well! This combination of fruity rasberry syrup, tart lime juice, and crisp ginger ale is a fun, crowd-pleasing mocktail you can serve year-round.

¾ ounce freshly squeezed lime juice

¾ ounce Berry Syrup (see page 159)

6 ounces ginger ale

1 ounce soda water

Mint sprig, for garnish

Raspberry, for garnish

Fill a highball glass with ice cubes. **Add** the lime juice and raspberry syrup to the glass and stir several times to chill. **Top** with the ginger ale and soda water and garnish with a mint sprig and a raspberry.

Celebrity-Inspired Mocktails

This chapter is full of fun and fancy nonalcoholic options, but I would be remiss if I didn't mention some tried-and-true booze-free beverages with celebrities' names.

ARNOLD PALMER: The golf pro's go-to beverage was a refreshing glass of 3 parts unsweetened iced tea and 1 part lemonade.

ROY ROGERS: Add a splash of pomegranate-flavored grenadine and a maraschino cherry garnish to classic cola, and you've got a soda kids and adults will love.

SHIRLEY TEMPLE: The world's first mocktail, this drink is a combination of grenadine, fresh lime juice, and ginger ale or lemon-lime soda. A garnish of a maraschino cherry (or three) is nonnegotiable.

ESSENTIAL TERMS

amaro/amari: Italian bitter liqueurs made from a variety of botanicals, traditionally consumed neat as a digestif and frequently used in cocktails (Amaro Montenegro, Cynar, and Amaro Averna).

aperitif: an alcoholic beverage served before a meal to whet the appetite. Aperitifs are often light and more dry than sweet (vermouth, white wine, Champagne, and Aperol Spritz [page 146]).

build: to "build" a cocktail is to create the drink in the glass in which it will be served (Dark 'n' Stormy [page 73]).

chaser/back: a beverage served alongside a cocktail or a shot that will follow the first drink. A glass of whiskey or Scotch served neat could be accompanied by a "water back."

digestif: an alcoholic beverage served after a meal to aid digestion (Cognac, sweet liqueurs, amari, and fortified wines).

dirty: to order a Martini "dirty" is to request the addition of a small amount of salty olive brine.

double-strain/fine-strain: pouring a cocktail through a fine-mesh strainer to catch any particles. It's called "double-straining" because the ice is strained with the Hawthorne strainer, and anything smaller is then strained out with the fine strainer.

dram: a small pour of whisky, most often Scotch or Irish. Technically speaking, a dram is ⅛ ounce, but "pouring a dram" means a small, most often unmeasured, single serving.

dry: liquors or cocktails that lack sweetness. A "dry" martini has less vermouth than usual, making it even more gin-forward.

float: a liquid (usually a spirit or bitters) that's carefully poured into the glass last, so that it floats on top of the cocktail. A Dark 'n' Stormy floats the base spirit on top of the mixer for visual effect.

long drink/tall drink: a mixed drink served in a tall glass with a mixer (Tom Collins [page 86]).

neat: a spirit or liqueur that is served at room temperature, without any ice or mixer.

on the rocks: a cocktail served over ice (Old Fashioned [page 99]).

pony: a "pony" refers to 1-ounce (or 30-mL) liquid measure.

roll or throw a cocktail: the middle ground between the subtlety of stirring and the vigorous action of shaking, which mixes well without as much dilution. To roll a drink, put ingredients with ice in a cocktail shaker and pour them from one tin to the other several times.

shaker tin: the larger metal shaker in a Boston shaker set. Many professional bartenders opt for two metal tins, rather than one metal and one glass. These are often referred to simply as "tins."

shooter: a short alcoholic beverage intended to be consumed in one go (or a "shot"). Shooters are often served as layered liquors and liqueurs.

split base: a cocktail with two or more primary liquors (Oaxacan Old Fashioned [page 122]).

swizzle: to churn a drink with a "swizzle stick." Swizzle sticks have tines on the bottom that extend in different directions, helping to thoroughly mix the drink. The drink is built in its glass and swizzled before serving.

up: a cocktail is shaken or stirred and then strained into a glass without ice (Martini [page 89]).

A BARTENDER'S MEASUREMENT CONVERSIONS

MEASUREMENT	IMPERIAL VOLUME	METRIC VOLUME
Dash	~10 drops	~1 mL
Bar spoon / teaspoon	⅙ ounce	5 mL
1½ teaspoons	¼ ounce	7.5 mL
Tablespoon	½ ounce	15 mL

MEASUREMENT CONVERSIONS

VOLUME EQUIVALENTS (LIQUID)

US STANDARD	US STANDARD (OUNCES)	METRIC (APPROXIMATE)
2 tablespoons	1 fl. oz.	30 mL
¼ cup	2 fl. oz.	60 mL
½ cup	4 fl. oz.	120 mL
1 cup	8 fl. oz.	240 mL
1½ cups	12 fl. oz.	355 mL
2 cups or 1 pint	16 fl. oz.	475 mL
4 cups or 1 quart	32 fl. oz.	1 L
1 gallon	128 fl. oz.	4 L

VOLUME EQUIVALENTS (DRY)

US STANDARD	METRIC (APPROXIMATE)
⅛ teaspoon	0.5 mL
¼ teaspoon	1 mL
½ teaspoon	2 mL
¾ teaspoon	4 mL
1 teaspoon	5 mL
1 tablespoon	15 mL
1 cup	235 mL

WEIGHT EQUIVALENTS

US STANDARD	METRIC (APPROXIMATE)
½ ounce	15 g
1 ounce	30 g
2 ounces	60 g
4 ounces	115 g
8 ounces	225 g
12 ounces	340 g
16 ounces or 1 pound	455 g

RESOURCES

WEBSITES

Cocktail Emporium: CocktailEmporium.com
Cocktail Kingdom: CocktailKingdom.com
Difford's Guide: DiffordsGuide.com
Imbibe: ImbibeMagazine.com
Punch: PUNCHDrink.com

BOOKS

Cocktail Codex by David Kaplan, Alex Day, and Nick Fauchald
Death & Co. by David Kaplan, Alex Day, and Nick Fauchald
Regarding Cocktails by Sasha Petraske and Georgette Moger-Petraske
The Savoy Cocktail Book by Harry Craddock

INDEX

A

Absinthe, 82, 98, 109, 140
Agave syrup, 114
Aged rum, 66, 128
Airmail, 149
Amy's Easy Crostini, 37
Aperol, 140
Aperol Spritz, 146
Arnold Palmer, 163

B

Balance and Columbian Repository, x
Bar area, 4
Bar spoons, 5, 7
Bars, fictional, 119
Bartender's Guide (Thomas), x
Base spirits, 26
Bergeron, Victor, 78, 124, 132, 133
Bermejo, Julio, 118

Bernice, 62
Berry, Jeff, 79
Berry Syrup, 159
Bitters, 22, 30, 82, 98, 140
Blenders, 6
Bloody Mary, 54–55
Bottoms Up (Saucier), 62
Boulevardier, 101
Bourbon, 103
    Boulevardier, 101
    Gold Rush, 106
    Manhattan, 100
    Mint Julep, 102
    Seelbach, 148
    Whiskey Smash, 105
    Whiskey Sour, 104
Bradsell, Dick, 58, 60, 61
Bramble, 91
Brandy, 127–128.
    See also Cognac
Brandy Alexander, 131
Brandy Old Fashioned, 130

C

Caipirovska, 57
Calvados, 128
Campari, 16
Cantarito, 120
Cape Codder, 53
Champagne, 17–18
    Airmail, 149
    Champagne Cocktail, 141
    Champagne Margarita, 145
    Death in the Afternoon, 151
    French 75, 142
    Old Cuban, 147
    Seelbach, 148
Champagne flutes, 8
Cheers, 119
Citrus juices, 18, 20
Citrus peels, 29
Citrus squeezers, 5, 7
Cleaning, 10
Clover Club, 90

Cocktail parties
  cleanup, 43
  don'ts, 38
  hosting, 41–43
  prepping for, 36
  setting up, 39, 41
  supplies, 38–40
Cocktails
  anatomy of, 26
  classifications of, 27
  common mistakes, 42
  history of, x–xi
Coffee liqueur, 50
Cognac, 14
  Brandy Alexander, 131
  Brandy Old
    Fashioned, 130
  Corpse Reviver #1, 134
  Fish House
    Punch, 136–137
  Japanese Cocktail, 135
  Scorpion, 132
  Sidecar, 129
Coleman, Ada, 92, 93
Corpse Reviver #1, 134
Corpse Reviver #2, 94
Cosmopolitan, 51
Coupe glasses, 8
Craddock, Harry, 45, 134
Crème de cacao, 114, 128

Crème de cassis, 50, 114
Cuba Libre, 67

D

Daiquiri, 70
Dark 'n' Stormy, 73
Death in the Afternoon, 151
Donn the Beachcomber, 78
DRINK (Gately), 150
Drinking songs, 144
Drunken Botanist, The
  (Stewart), 150
Dry-shaking, 28

E

Earl Grey Cobbler, 157
Easy Bloody Mary Mix, 55
Edible flowers, 154
El Diablo, 124
El Presidente, 72
Espresso Martini, 61

F

Fernet branca, 82, 98
Fish House Punch, 136–137
Fitzgerald, F. Scot, 150

Flavorings, 21–22, 30
Fortified wines, 17–18
French 75, 142

G

Galliano, 50
Garnishes, 21–22,
  29–30, 154
Gately, Iain, 150
Gimlet, 84
Gin, 13, 81–82
  Bramble, 91
  Clover Club, 90
  Corpse Reviver #2, 94
  French 75, 142
  Gimlet, 84
  Gin and Tonic, 83
  Hanky Panky, 92
  Jasmine, 88
  Martini, 89
  Negroni, 87
  Ramos Gin Fizz, 95
  Tom Collins, 86
Ginger Limeade, 160–161
Glassware, 8–9
Gold Rush, 106
Grenadine, 66, 114

H

Hacks
  glassware, 9
  tools, 7
Hangover cures, 44–45
Hanky Panky, 92
Harrington, Paul, 88
Hemingway, Ernest, 68, 151
Herbs, clapping, 30
Highball cocktails, 27
Highball glasses, 8, 9
Honey Syrup, 75
How to Mix Drinks
  (Thomas), 104, 135

I

Ice, 15
IMBIBE! (Wondrich), 150
Intoxica! (Berry), 79

J

Japanese Cocktail, 135
Jasmine, 88
Jiggers, 5, 7
Jungle Bird, 79

K

Knives, 6

L

Layering, 29
Leaky Cauldron, The, 119
Lemon Drop, 56
Lemons, 18, 20, 21
Lillet blanc, 82
Limes, 18, 20, 21
Liqueurs, 16.
  See also specific
Liquors, 13–14, 40.
  See also specific

M

Mai Tai, 77
Manhattan, 100
Margarita, 116–117
  Champagne
    Margarita, 145
  Tommy's Margarita, 118
Martini, 89
  Espresso Martini, 61
Menocal, Mario García, 72

Mezcal, 114, 123
Mint, 21
Mint Julep, 102
Missionary's Downfall, 74
Mixers, 18–19
Mocktails, 153–154, 163
  Earl Grey Cobbler, 157
  Ginger Limeade, 160–161
  Spicy Mock-scow
    Mule, 156
  Strawberry-Lavender
    Soda, 158
  Virgin Floradora, 162
  Virgin Piña Colada, 155
Modifiers, 26
Moe's Tavern, 119
Mojito, 68–69
Moscow Mule, 52
  Spicy Mock-scow
    Mule, 156
Mos Eisley Cantina, 119
Muddlers, 6, 7
Muddling, 29

N

Negroni, 87
Negroni Sbagliato, 143

O

Oaxacan Old
    Fashioned, 122
Old Cuban, 147
Old Fashioned, 99
    Brandy Old
        Fashioned, 130
    Oaxacan Old
        Fashioned, 122
Old fashioned cocktails, 27
Old Pal, 107
On Booze (Fitzgerald), 150
Ong, Jeffrey, 79
Orange bitters, 82
Orange blossom water, 82
Oranges, 18, 20, 21
Orgeat, 66, 128
Oxford Night Caps, x

P

Paddy's Pub, 119
Painkiller, 76
Paloma, 115
Peach liqueur, 66, 128
Peychaud, Antoine, 108
Peychaud's bitters, 98, 140
Piña Colada, 71
    Virgin Piña Colada, 155

Prosecco, 18
    Aperol Spritz, 146
    Negroni Sbagliato, 143

R

Ramos Gin Fizz, 95
Rinsing, 30
Robertson, William, 107
Rocks glasses, 8, 9
Roy Rogers, 163
Rum, 13, 65–66
    Airmail, 149
    Cuba Libre, 67
    Daiquiri, 70
    Dark 'n' Stormy, 73
    El Presidente, 72
    Fish House
        Punch, 136–137
    Jungle Bird, 79
    Mai Tai, 77
    Missionary's Downfall, 74
    Mojito, 68–69
    Old Cuban, 147
    Painkiller, 76
    Piña Colada, 71
    Scorpion, 132
Russian Spring
    Punch, 58–59

Rye whiskey, 98, 103
    Old Pal, 107
    Sazerac, 108
    Toronto, 110
    Whiskey Sour, 104

S

Saucier, Ted, 62
Saunders, Audrey, 147
Savoy Cocktail Book, The
    (Craddock), 45, 134
Sazerac, 108
Scorpion, 132
Scotch, 103
Seasonings, 26
Seelbach, 148
Shakers, 5, 7
Shaking, 28
Shelf life
    fortified and sparkling
        wines, 18
    liqueurs, 16
    liquors, 14
    mixers, 19
Shirley Temple, 163
Sidecar, 129
Siegel, T. J., 106
Silk Stocking, 125
Simple Syrup, 85

INDEX

Sodas, 19

Sour cocktails, 27

Sparkling wines, 17–18,
    139–140. *See also*
    Champagne; Prosecco
    Death in the
        Afternoon, 151
    Negroni Sbagliato, 143
    Old Cuban, 147
    Russian Spring
        Punch, 58–59
    Seelbach, 148

Spicy Mock-scow Mule, 156

Spirit forward cocktails, 27

Stewart, Amy, 150

Stirring, 28

Storage
    fortified and sparkling
        wines, 18
    liqueurs, 4, 16
    liquors, 4, 14
    mixers, 19

Strainers, 5, 6, 7

Strawberry-Lavender
    Soda, 158

Straws, 154

Syrups, 19, 114
    Berry Syrup, 159
    Honey Syrup, 75
    Simple Syrup, 85

Strawberry-Lavender
    Syrup, 158

T

Tequila, 14, 113–114
    Cantarito, 120
    Champagne
        Margarita, 145
    El Diablo, 124
    Margarita, 116–117
    Oaxacan Old
        Fashioned, 122
    Paloma, 115
    Silk Stocking, 125
    Tequila Sunrise, 121
    Tommy's
        Margarita, 118

Thomas, Jerry, x, 104, 135

Tiki cocktails, 27, 78

Tom Collins, 86

Tommy's Margarita, 118

Tools, 4–7

Toronto, 110

Trader Vic. *See*
    Bergeron, Victor

Triple sec, 16

Tropical
    cocktails, 27

V

Vegetable peelers, 6

Vermouth, dry, 17–18

Vermouth, sweet, 17–18

Virgin Floradora, 162

Virgin Piña Colada, 155

Vodka, 13, 49–50
    Bernice, 62
    Bloody Mary, 54–55
    Caipirovska, 57
    Cape Codder, 53
    Cosmopolitan, 51
    Espresso Martini, 61
    Lemon Drop, 56
    Moscow Mule, 52
    Russian Spring
        Punch, 58–59

W

Washington, George, 65

Whip-shaking, 28

Whiskey, 14, 97–98, 103.
    See also Bourbon; Rye
    whiskey; Scotch
    Old Fashioned, 99

Whiskey Smash, 105

Whiskey Sour, 104

Wineglasses, 9

Wondrich, David, 72, 150

ABOUT THE AUTHOR

 **Amy Traynor** is an award-winning cocktail blogger and photographer. Her blog, Moody Mixologist, was the recipient of the 2018 SAVEUR Magazine Best Drinks Blog Award. She holds a BFA in photography from the School of Visual Arts in New York City. Her photography has been exhibited internationally and featured in several publications, including *Story Gourmet*. Amy resides in New Hampshire with her husband and daughters.

CPSIA information can be obtained
at www.ICGtesting.com
Printed in the USA
JSHW050803031022
31149JS00002B/2